FUND RAISERS That Work

by
Margaret Hinchey
and
dozens of contributors

Loveland, CO

Fund Raisers That Work

Copyright © 1988 by Thom Schultz Publications, Inc.

Second Printing

Credits
Edited by Lane Eskew
Designed by Judy Atwood
Illustrations by Jean Bruns, Martin Bucella, Rand Kruback, Jan Knudson and Alan Wilkes

Library of Congress Cataloging-in-Publication Data
Fund raisers that work
    p.   cm.
  ISBN 0-931529-33-6 (pbk.)
  1. Church work with teenagers. 2. Church work with youth.
3. Church fund raising. I. Eskew, Lane.
BV4447.F86 1988   88-15703
254.8—dc19   CIP

Printed in the United States of America

Contents

$ervices 57

$pecial Events 77

Introduction

Fund Raising: A Mixed Blessing
(Or, "We've Got to Raise How Much?")

The scene is the same in churches of different denominations across the country. There's a special youth trip or activity coming up, and it takes money to make it happen. Where do you begin?

Somehow it would be easier to simply assess each young person going on the trip his or her share of the expenses. But ease *isn't* the name of the game. In fact, the positives of active and creative fund raising far outweigh the negatives of the time and trouble you might incur. In the following pages, you'll discover information and tips on how to raise funds with your youth group. You'll also find out how to create a positive attitude and establish a game plan to help everyone involved become excited about your youth group fund raisers.

Why Bother With Fund Raisers?

Fund raisers are usually thought of as having only one purpose: accumulating funds for a specific project. If that's the case, then you can probably assume there are several other ways to finance a project. For example:

1. Your congregation may simply decide to take the needed funds out of the church treasury.

2. The youth group may plan far enough in advance so the youth activity can become a part of the church budget for the coming year.

3. Each young person or parent who plans to participate in the project may be assessed a portion of the costs for the event.

4. Monthly dues may be charged to youth group members and placed in the youth group treasury to finance upcoming events.

5. Grants, scholarships or matching funds from benevolent

organizations or companies are possible, especially for service-related projects.

6. Direct donations may be solicited from members or friends of the church.

As you can see, fund raising isn't the only way to meet financial goals. Propose some of the preceding suggestions as alternatives to fund raising or suggest they be used in combination with the fund-raising projects.

If other options run out or they're simply not feasible for your group, it's time to rely on fund raising to secure the necessary funds to do the ministry you choose. Most church members are eager to support their youth groups by buying products or participating in special fund-raising activities. It's helpful, however, to establish some criteria to help focus your fund-raising projects.

Criteria for Using Fund Raisers

Your youth group members may want to establish some guidelines or criteria for the fund raisers they plan. On the next page is a checklist of possible criteria to consider before you begin fund raising. Duplicate this checklist and have both young people and adults complete it. Hold a meeting to discuss criteria and examine potential fund raisers while using the list. If you publish the checklist ahead of time, in a newsletter or in a bulletin, all of the congregation will have an understanding of the forethought and planning that have gone into your fund-raising efforts.

This checklist may only be a beginning, depending on the constitution of your youth group and church. It will, however, open the door to healthy discussions about purposes for fund raisers as well as give ownership to others. It may also assure you that everyone has a common understanding of the purpose of your fund raising.

Dos and Don'ts of Fund Raising

Before proceeding with fund raising, consider the following:

1. Do begin your planning well in advance of the event. Al-

Fund-Raising Checklist

Our youth group fund raisers should:

_____ 1. Directly benefit both the youth group and the individual who is purchasing our services.

_____ 2. Reach out to serve another's needs as we fulfill our own; that is, be "other-directed" as well as "us-directed."

_____ 3. Give a portion of the profits to a worthy cause outside the group.

_____ 4. Sell an item or service that the buyer needs.

_____ 5. Be divided between whole group efforts and individual projects.

_____ 6. Be selected by both the youth group and the advisers.

_____ 7. Be voted upon and approved by parents of the young people.

_____ 8. Be approved by the pastor.

_____ 9. Be approved by the church council (or other governing body).

_____ 10. Be limited to _____ (number of) fund-raising projects per year.

_____ 11. Be fun as well as work.

_____ 12. Other: _____.

Permission to photocopy this handout granted for local church use only.
Copyright © 1988 by Group Books, Inc., Box 481, Loveland, CO 80539.

low at least twice as much time as you think you will need.

2. Don't wait until the last minute to solicit adult help. Ask parents and other adults to get involved during the beginning

stages of planning.

3. *Do* be selfish. Consider your own schedule in the plans.

4. *Don't* forget the busy lives of your teenagers. Remember to consider their schedules.

5. *Do* give ownership to young people, parents and other adults by seeking their advice, assistance and support from the start.

6. *Don't* assume anything. Figure all costs of a project at their highest potential. It's better to be surprised if there's extra money left rather than disappointed because the project costs more than you expected.

7. *Do* be creative. Think of every possible angle of support for your young people. Consider every way to get what you need.

8. *Don't* move ahead with a project without proper approval from your church council or governing board. Use the channels your church has established.

9. *Do* keep people informed. Make sure the congregational members, staff, parents and young people are fully aware of the projects, the expectations, the goals and the time frame for every event.

10. *Don't* forget to pray for your young people and the benefits they can receive through the fund-raising projects as well as the events they are raising money for.

11. *Do* help young people see a purpose in their projects other than simply raising funds for their event.

12. *Don't* build failure into projects by neglecting publicity, planning and adequate personnel to carry out the event.

13. *Do* thank people who assist your projects—young people, adults and businesses who donate goods and services. Everyone enjoys appreciation, whether it be public or private.

14. *Don't* forget to have fun!

Developing a Planning Calendar

One way to avoid communication breakdowns and missed goals is to establish a planning calendar. Develop the calendar in a way that it can be duplicated for your young people, parents and church staff. (Group Books has a convenient *Youth Ministry Clip Art Calendar* that can be duplicated each month.

All you need to do is fill in the dates of projects, deadlines and meetings.)

The amount of lead time and the number of fund raisers you will need depend upon the amount of money your group needs. For example, taking 10 young people on an overnight retreat at $25 per person means you'll only need to raise $250. Many single fund raisers included in this book can produce such funds. But if you plan to take 30 young people across the country to a summer event in Colorado, you'll have a different situation to address. With an estimate of $400 per person, you'll need to raise $12,000, which could take several months and involve several fund-raising projects. So start planning now . . .

Steps in the Planning Process

1. Consult your pastor about the activity you want to support with fund raising. If you don't have the support of your pastor and the rest of the church staff, you'll be fighting an uphill battle even before fund raising begins. (This includes the person who types the bulletin and the newsletters into which much of your publicity goes!)

2. Get approval from the proper church board or committee for the trip or event you're planning. A clear understanding of your intent will stifle criticism and skepticism about your fund-raising efforts.

3. Meet with the youth board, including counselors and officers of the youth group. Make sure leaders support the event you're promoting. This support includes a commitment to have adequate adult supervision and participation of officers at the event and at the fund raisers.

4. Form a fund-raising planning committee from your youth group and adult leadership. Make sure individuals on the committee have gifts that relate to fund raising as well as creativity and wisdom. Don't just pick friends or people you like!

5. Write a job description for the committee. Include necessary timetables and goals. Make sure everyone knows this group is a *planning* committee so its members aren't expected to do all the fund raising themselves.

6. Organize a fun, informative evening for the entire youth

group and their parents. Discuss the event being planned and ask the fund-raising planning committee to make an initial report about how funds can be raised to support the activity. If promotional videos, slides and other media are available, be sure to have them on hand to "sell" the idea. This kind of report will give added impetus to the suggested fund raisers. Invite questions and be prepared to answer them or find out the answers as soon as possible.

7. Ask youth group members and their parents to talk about the activity at home. Give each group member a commitment form. Have them complete the form, indicating their interest in the activity and their willingness to participate in the planning and execution of fund raisers to support the activity.

8. Set a deadline for returning the commitment forms. Once you have the number of people identified, you can start to plan your fund raisers.

Use of a Fund-Raising Planning Committee

Once you've gained approval and support from church leaders, adult counselors and young people, the fun begins. Encourage members of your fund-raising planning committee to be creative.

Plan an evening of brainstorming with your fund-raising committee, adult counselors and other key leaders. Suggest to the committee that they invite congregational members who are experienced with fund raising for civic or business organizations. Ask different youth leaders to read a portion of this book ahead of time and be prepared to offer two or three fund-raising suggestions they like from each section. Ask them to share in detail the purpose, expectations and desired results of each fund raiser. Tape newsprint to the walls of your meeting room and list possible fund raisers. Remember: In brainstorming, people do not express opinions—yet.

After the creativity of your group is exhausted and the list has been made, divide fund raisers into three categories: sales, services and special events. Decide which suggestions are feasible for your group.

Give each person a means for voting on the fund raisers he or she believes are the best. You can do this with a show of hands, a secret ballot or even the dot method. (For the dot method, purchase colored, self-sticking dots from your local office supply store. Buy two or three different colors. Give individuals the same number of dots and allow them to vote by placing their dots on the newsprint sheets. If you choose to use more than one color of dots, you might give instructions such as the following: "The bright orange dots indicate 'This fund raiser looks great,' the blue dots represent 'I don't think this one is too hot' and the brown dots say 'Yuck, I don't think we should even suggest this one.'" This method of voting gives a quick visual approach to feelings about the top fund raisers.)

Have the committee take the final list of suggested fund raisers to the next youth group meeting for approval. It might be wise to choose three times as many fund raisers as you actually intend to use so youth group members can provide input and feel like they're part of the decision. Have committee members prepare to discuss the following about each fund-raising idea:

1. Purpose of the fund raiser.
2. How it will be carried out.
3. Needs and time expectations.
4. Anticipated income.

After committee members have offered their suggestions and responded to group members' questions and concerns, ask for approval from the group. Use one of the methods suggested before. Ask the fund-raising planning committee to take the group members' responses to formulate a fund-raising plan for presentation at the next meeting.

Forming a Fund-Raising Game Plan

Much of the success for your fund raising depends upon timing. For example, three sales fund raisers during the month of January, after people have spent their money on Christmas presents, followed by two months with no fund raisers indicates poor planning. Allow time between fund raisers and vary the nature of the projects among sales, services and special events. If you choose six fund raisers to support an activity, try to have a balance between those three categories.

Remember, certain projects are seasonal. A 1950s Drive-In is great fun. But if you live in Minnesota, you'd better plan to have it during a summer month! Fertilizer sales work great in the spring, rummage sales fare well in fall, and Christmas wreaths sell best in November and December. For everything (including fund-raising projects) there is a season.

Group or Individual Projects?

It's important to think about the nature of your young people. Face it, some kids just aren't salespeople. Some teenagers would rather die before they ask someone to buy their product. This means that if a young person is to profit from a sales fund raiser, Mom or Dad will probably take the product to work and sell it to people there. On the other hand, that same young person might have tremendous talent at putting together a great talent show, publicizing an event or helping with a fellowship night at church.

Strive for a balance between group projects (everyone works together and divides the profits) and individual projects (the individual reaps the benefits of his or her own initiative and/or selling capacity). Some examples from this book include the following:

Group Projects
1950s Drive-In (page 59)
All-Night Bake Sale
  (page 34)
Singing Mom-a-Grams
  (page 93)

Individual Projects
Business Carwash (page 59)
Fertilizer Sale (page 45)
Historic Note Cards (page 87)

Alternating group projects and individual projects on a monthly basis can benefit your group. Begin with a whole group project so everyone's account will register an amount in the ledger. For example, if you're planning for a special event in July, you might schedule your fund raisers like this:

Month	Event	Distribution of profits
January	Chili-Making Fun	Group accounts
February	Light Bulb Sale	Individual accounts
March	All-Night Bake Sale	Group accounts
April	Fertilizer Sale	Individual accounts
May	Singing Mom-a-Grams	Group accounts
June	Cinnamon Roll Sale	Individual accounts
July	1950s Drive-In	Group accounts

Group projects. Establish guidelines ahead of time that explain clearly how profits from a given project will be divided. For example, if your youth group sponsors a Parents' Day Off, decide whether anyone who works that day will get an equal share of the profits. Consider people who only work part of a day or merely help with publicity and scheduling. The fund-raising planning committee and adult youth group leaders should address the questions early. After devising an equitable formula for dividing funds, the committee must publicize and maintain its position so group members will understand what's going on.

Individual projects. Every group has a few "go-getters" who can sell anything to anybody. (Their relatives, friends and neighbors usually have closets full of calendars, candy bars and Christmas ornaments they've purchased from the go-getters!) If one of your youth group members is particularly good at sales, ask that person to share his or her techniques with the others. Have that individual give a sales demonstration or tutor the less-eager salespeople in the group. Check to see if this supersalesperson would be willing to go with others and coach them on their door-to-door efforts.

When planning fund raisers, remember sales are much easier if items are similar to what buyers would purchase anyway. Think about selling household items such as soap, food products and gifts. Novelties and more frivolous items are easier for buyers to resist. Picking the wrong item to sell only wastes time. Suggest to young people that they select items that are useful to their buyers. Easy sales boost not only sales but the egos of the sellers.

Combination. Some events may combine group and individual projects. For example, group members may take individual orders for pizzas, then get together on a Sunday afternoon to make pizzas and deliver them. In that case, a percentage of the profits could go to the individual sellers and a percentage to those who make and deliver the pizza creations.

The "Free" Carwash (a variation of the Business Carwash, page 59) also has benefits for the group as well as individuals. Before the project, individuals can seek pledges from individuals or businesses for the number of cars the group will wash. Those car owners who haven't made a pledge but just "show up" at the carwash may choose to make a donation to the group. These donations can be divided among all car washers who worked the day of the project.

It's possible that through combined individual projects and group projects some individuals may raise their share of the funds early. If this happens, young people should agree on how to handle this situation before it becomes a problem. For example, your committee might establish a policy in which individuals who reach their goal would be encouraged to participate and help others in group projects, but their share of the profits would be divided among the others until all members have reached their goal. When everyone reaches the goal, use the additional profits for paying the way of adult leaders, planning a surprise stop on the trip or contributing to a worthy cause.

Accounting Procedures

No matter what size group or what amount of money you're working with, you should have accurate and fair accounting procedures for fund raisers. This may be the first time your young people have dealt with money that isn't solely their own. Through supervision and proper advice, they can learn proper budgeting and accounting procedures that will help them through a lifetime.

Once it's been established who will attend an event and benefit from fund raisers, set up a ledger that includes all names of young people who plan to participate. Include space to record the names of fund raisers, date of projects and the amounts to be attributed to each individual. (Or use the Fund-Raising Accountability Form in *Fast Forms for Youth Ministry* from Group Books.) Following is an example:

Event: National Christian Youth Congress
Number to attend: four

Fund raiser ➡	Chili-Making Fun	Light Bulb Sale
Date ➡	January 15	February 21
Total amount earned		
(after expenses) ➡	$189.36	$148.00
Amount to individual ➡	$ 47.34	(Individual)
Group		
Janie Anderson ➡	$ 47.34	$ 40.00
Anita Garrett ➡	$ 47.34	$ 20.00
David Manson ➡	$ 47.34	$ 88.00
Gary Rodman ➡	$ 47.34	-0-

Establish a special bank account for the trip or event you're supporting. Your treasurer should be able to balance the money in that special account and the amounts attributed to each individual at any given time.

At no time is it wise to give cash profits from a fund raiser directly to the young people. Individuals or businesses who donate to a special cause expect the money to go to that project. Money distributed in cash tempts young people to spend the money in other ways such as on a new tape or a chocolate sundae. Use an accounting system that credits accounts and maintains all money in one account.

If you're involved in a project that requires earning large amounts of money, it would be wise to invest that money in an interest-bearing account. When it comes time to withdraw the money for your event, you can use the accumulated interest for a special treat along the way. This interest can also be an incentive for groups to get started early on their fund-raising projects.

Another Key to Success: Preparation

In order for your fund raising to be successful, adequate

and appropriate, preparations are essential for each project.
Make sure information about fund-raising projects reach three
different groups of people: your youth group members, your
congregation and at times your community.

Obviously, you can't make a fund-raising project successful
by yourself. This is a "youth fund raiser," not a "youth group
leader's fund raiser." Guard against failure by making sure
youth group members plan and carry out the event themselves. Include these ingredients as part of every fund raiser:

1. Appropriate preparation of materials and facilities.
2. Sufficient help to carry out the activity.
3. Adequate adult supervision.

Ask young people and adults to sign up well in advance of
any project. When they commit themselves to a project, let
them know what is expected, especially time commitment, the
tasks to be done and, if possible, the hours they'll be expected to work. The more information you provide ahead of time,
the better off you'll be in having a successful fund raiser.

Depending on your system of organization, consider having
a young person and an adult co-chair each fund-raising
project. This team would be responsible for making sure all
preparations are made and executed on time and in the
proper manner. This would include providing publicity, secur-
ing needed assistance, assigning jobs, setting expectations and
designating any other tasks necessary to accomplish this
specific fund raiser.

Preparation of Materials and Facility

When planning a fund raiser, make a list of all the items you
will need. For example, if you're having a spaghetti dinner,
make a grocery list of all food items, paper products and
other goods several weeks in advance. Watch newspaper ads
and coupons for special deals so you're not scrambling at the
last minute to get bargains for the youth group. Talk with
businesses or organizations who've offered assistance about
donating items you might need.

Involve kids in the shopping trip to purchase items for the
fund raiser. This can be a great learning experience for young
people as they are forced to compare items when they shop,

buy in quantities and plan for a large event. Make sure a knowledgeable adult accompanies the young people on their buying trip.

One youth group leader helped the kids prepare a grocery list for a spaghetti supper for 100 people at their church. When the list was complete, the youth leader noticed she had failed to suggest some quantities for the young shoppers. But they assured their leader they knew what they were doing and left for the store. The kids returned from their shopping adventure with 100 pounds of spaghetti noodles—1 pound per person!—and 1 gallon of ice cream—1 spoonful per person! The young people thought they had done a great job because they'd spent less than the youth leader had budgeted for the supper.

When making plans for a fund-raising event to be held in your church or some facility outside your church, make sure you book that location far in advance. Church calendars fill quickly, and some groups may assume they can use facilities without actually receiving permission. Make sure your date and the number of hours you use it for (including setup and cleanup times) are scheduled through the proper church channels.

If you are using facilities outside your church such as a community building or booth at an indoor flea market, a deposit or fee may be required. Be sure you're aware of all requirements and regulations regarding the use of this space before you make any commitments. Arrange to pick up the keys and find out how the facility is to be cleaned when the event is over.

Sufficient Help to Carry Out the Activity

Achieving a proper balance between helpers and tasks to be accomplished is often difficult. Try to outline all tasks needed for a specific fund raiser. Then estimate the number of people needed to accomplish each task. (Keeping accurate records from year to year, especially if a specific fund raiser is repeated, can be extremely helpful in this part of the planning process.) Ask the youth group members to sign up in advance for a task that best meets their talents and a time that meets their schedule.

Having too many helpers can often be as detrimental as having too few. Too many people in a kitchen, for example, decreases the productivity, quality and efficiency of those who could adequately accomplish the tasks on their own. Also, not everyone is good at everything. Encourage young people to pursue tasks they know how to do or are willing and able to learn. If training is necessary, make sure there's a knowledgeable instructor and adequate time for training to take place.

Adequate Adult Supervision

If you're the youth leader, you will burn out quickly if you take primary responsibility for organizing and carrying out all fund raisers for your youth group. This is an excellent area to give ownership and responsibility to parents. Personally solicit their support and assistance for any fund-raising projects. Since communication between young people and their parents sometimes breaks down, parents may not realize they've been "volunteered." Avoid that uncomfortable situation by double-checking with parents. Depending on the number of fund raisers and the number of parents available, consider asking each parent to assume primary responsibility for one fund raiser and to serve as an adult adviser for another.

If more adult support is needed, don't forget the available resources you have in your congregation. Involve the senior citizens group in making food for a bake sale or creating Christmas wreaths. Many senior citizens are active, vibrant and capable people with years of experience. Young adults provide another source of energy and talent. Use them as drivers for events, mentors or simply encouragers for those who are wilting over a hot grill.

Every congregation has individuals with special gifts and skills—carpenters, chefs, writers and photographers. Don't be afraid to ask these skilled individuals to teach others or donate their time. Most churches have time and talent records available in which you can look for specific skills if you aren't aware of the gifts within your congregation.

When you use these individuals—parents, senior citizens, young adults or people with special gifts and abilities—don't forget to thank them for their services. Have your fund-raising planning committee assign a person to write thank-you notes to all non-youth group participants in each specific project. Include individuals and/or businesses who donate their time, products, advertising space or anything else you use in your fund raiser.

It's also important to thank people publicly for their services. If you're having a dinner, schedule a "cooks parade" at the event. If there's a printed program, list with a note of appreciation the names of those who've donated time, products or services. If your church uses Sunday bulletins or newsletters, acknowledge people who helped make your fund raiser a success. People like to be appreciated, and they'll be encouraged to help again when asked. Some might even volunteer next time.

Publicity to Your Congregation

For most youth group fund-raising activities, the principal supporters of the project will probably be members of your congregation. In addition to the more traditional means of communication such as newsletters, bulletins and posters around the church, use your creativity to think of new ways to keep people informed.

Before you begin asking for money, let the congregation members know about the activity they're going to be asked to support. Tell them when the event will take place, where it will be, what the purpose is and who will be participating in it. By sharing this information *before* you begin asking for money, people will have a vision for the event and have more interest in supporting it. You can probably share this information at the same time you are soliciting adult involvement with the youth group. By sharing the event with the whole congregation, you may reach some inactive young people who would like to join the action. As you know the details of the event, write an article for the newsletter or bulletin. Or prepare a special letter that can be mailed at a bulk rate to the whole congregation.

When the time comes to schedule fund raisers for the event, let church members know well in advance so they don't purchase that item or service from another source. For example, a church member might purchase a Christmas wreath from a local greenhouse because he or she didn't realize the youth group would be taking orders the next Sunday.

10 Quick, Creative and Money-Saving Publicity Tips

1. Use eye-catching teasers and gimmicks in Sunday bulletins and church newsletters. For example, several weeks before an event, ask the church secretary to intersperse lines throughout the bulletin like the following:

● "F.L.Y.S.S.A.T.S. is coming!" (First Lutheran Youth Spaghetti Supper and Talent Show.)

● "Have you heard what's happening on April 9? Details to follow in next week's newsletter."

● "Don't miss the F.A.P.A.P.E. !" (First Annual Pizza and Pop Extravaganza.)

2. Arrange for special clip art to highlight bulletin and newsletter articles. (Group Books has two great books you can use: *Youth Ministry Clip Art* and *Outrageous Clip Art for Youth Ministry*.) Ask a talented artist in your youth group to design a logo to go with your event.

3. After the congregation is informed about your event, prepare a special fund raiser and insert a coupon in the newsletter that says something like the following:

● "Fifty cents off the $3 admission to the youth group's Talent Show!"

● "A family discount! Bring five people with the same last name to the youth group's Italian Dinner, and you can bring *a sixth person free.*"

● "Bring four people who live in the same house to the melodrama—and you can bring a neighbor for half-price!

Most people are attracted to a bargain and will give some thought to taking advantage of a special deal.

4. Invest in a button maker. (Available from Badg-A-Minit, DEPT. GP388, 348 N. 30th Rd., La Salle, IL 61301.) Buttons

are a great way to personalize your projects. Use acronyms that will cause people to ask about the button you are wearing. For example, "CYO is selling S.S.S." (Catholic Youth Organization is selling Super Submarine Sandwiches).

The button maker itself can be used as a fund raiser. Use it for making personalized buttons at Christmas, St. Valentine's Day, Easter, Mother's Day or other special occasions.

5. Use theme items on posters to catch people's attention. If you're having a bake sale, glue a slice of bread, a paper cupcake liner, a wooden spoon or a cookie to the sign. If you're having a newspaper drive, cover a piece of tagboard with old newspapers and use big, black letters written on the newspaper to give the information.

6. Use theme projects to help publicize the event you're raising money for. For example, if you're going on a mission project to Mexico, sponsor a Mexican fiesta with Mexican food, piñatas and music as a fellowship activity. For the price of admission, you could offer a certain number of tickets that would be good for cakewalks, fishponds, piñatas and other games for the whole family. You could sell additional tickets for a nominal price as well.

7. Solicit donations from people in order to get a commitment. Rather than sell tickets for an Easter breakfast, for example, ask people to sign up to bring items and take a freewill offering at the door. Post a chart on the bulletin board that instructs people to sign up below if they plan to attend. They should sign their name under the product they plan to bring. Remind them to list quantities. Here's an example of a chart:

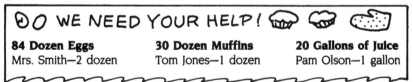

🐥🐣 WE NEED YOUR HELP! 🧁 🍞 🍞		
84 Dozen Eggs	**30 Dozen Muffins**	**20 Gallons of Juice**
Mrs. Smith—2 dozen	Tom Jones—1 dozen	Pam Olson—1 gallon

This method helps to offset costs, allows people to contribute more than they might if they bought a ticket and gives people ownership and commitment in advance of the event. Remember to list the donors and add a word of thanks in the next newsletter.

8. Recycle items from your local stores and businesses for

your events. Most businesses spend a great deal of money on signs and advertising gimmicks that they use for only a season. If you see a display or a hanging advertisement in your local store, ask the merchant if you may have it when he or she is finished using it. Let him know you will come by and pick it up and be there when you say you will.

Grocery stores or movie theaters sometimes have life-size caricatures of famous personalities endorsing products or selling movies. Ask the manager if your non-profit organization can have the cardboard display figure when the promotion is over. What better way to advertise your event than to have a celebrity endorsement in the halls of your church!

9. Drawings or raffles for special projects are great attractions to use for your publicity. If you need tickets or coupons, it's not necessary to spend lots of money to have them reproduced. Most church copy machines can produce sheets of tickets at a relatively low cost. If you need consecutive numbering or two halves numbered, put some of your young people to work with a pen. If perforations are required (for two halves of a raffle ticket or for coupons), a sewing machine and a steady hand can get the job done quickly. A heavy-duty sewing machine needle (without the thread) can pierce holes in a straight line through a small stack of regular paper. (Don't use heavy paper or cardboard, or you'll have the expense of replacing the sewing machine!)

10. Ask some of your talented youth group members to prepare a brief, humorous skit that promotes your upcoming fund raiser. Involve others in your skit such as chairpeople of various committees, parents, adult choir members, young adults and senior citizens. Or, have youth group members prepare a devotional with a theme relating to the activity they're raising money for. Arrange for the young people to share that devotional as an opening for several boards, committees or organizations in a particular month.

Publicity in Your Community

In addition to the suggestions made for publicity to the congregation, there are vehicles that can reach people in the surrounding community. Use a variety of media to capture people's attention at different times and in different places, to increase curiosity about an event and to make people want to become part of the action. Here are some tips:

1. Radio and TV stations are required by law to give a certain amount of free air-time to community concerns. Check with your local stations to see if your group's project qualifies. Ask for advice from the advertising people at the station in order to prepare your advertising copy. Select your best speakers and help them practice for their presentation. Ask your local radio and TV stations to publicize your fund raisers and events on their community calendars. Find out their deadlines and get your information to them well in advance.

2. Local newspapers usually have a "What's Happening This Week in _____" section also. Send them complete information in advance of the deadline and give your phone number in case they have questions or the information is unclear.

3. Newspapers often have religion sections in which they feature full-length articles about activities in the community's churches. Have one of your youth group members who has a flair for writing develop a story and submit it to that section of the paper. (Be sure you read the article to check for accuracy before you deliver it to the paper.) Include a picture from last year's event, or stage a picture of what's going to happen this year. This extra touch will add appeal to the article.

4. If your project is actually a service—especially if it has an unusual twist like the "Youth Sponsor *Free* Carwash" (variation of Business Carwash, page 59)—you may have the potential to attract on-the-spot media coverage for the 6 o'clock news or a feature in the newspaper. People are always excited about human interest stories.

5. Grocery stores and other businesses often allow you to place signs or posters on a bulletin board or in a window. Make sure you include the name of the church and its location. Remember to write the date your sign can be removed on the back or have group members pick up or remove signs after the event is over. This courtesy helps businesses keep a positive attitude about this service they provide.

6. Display signs on the church lawn or string banners across

the front of the church (make sure this form of publicity is approved by the proper individuals or committees of your church). These vivid reminders are great ways to let the neighborhood know what is happening.

7. Distribute fliers or door hangers around the neighborhood adjacent to the church or in a housing area where your members live. These notices are another means of informing non-members about an event. Remind the young people distributing the fliers to place them in or on the door since placing items in mailboxes is a federal offense.

8. Kites, hot-air balloons, spotlights, neon signs or unique vehicles parked on the curb with a special sign are more expensive forms of publicity, but they are excellent ways of drawing attention to a special event at your church. Use your imagination!

Publicity can make the difference in a successful event; however, it doesn't happen without some creativity, planning and effort. Use your resources and enlist the help of others. You'll make your efforts worthwhile.

Step-by-Step Planning for a 1950s Drive-In Fund Raiser

(This event is described on page 59.)

Two months before the event.

Explain the event to the pastor and select an open date on the church calendar. A weekend night is probably best. Sunday nights are often good since you have a last chance at publicity on Sunday morning, and people are less likely to forget if they're reminded the day of the event. Make sure this is a free night on the calendar because you'll use the whole parking lot.

One month before the event.

1. Have your young people make posters reflecting the '50s theme for the night. Include items from the menu, hours and location of the activity. Highlight the unique experience of being served hamburgers and other drive-in items by bubble-gum-chewing, roller-skating carhops. Since this event could appeal to people outside your church, make enough signs to

post in local businesses and at church.

2. The unusual nature of this back-to-the-'50s activity could attract the news media. Make sure you alert radio, TV and newspaper reporters to this fun evening sponsored by the young people of your church. Put the information on the community calendars provided by the different media.

3. Solicit the aid of carhops who know how to roller-skate. Other young people and adults can serve as cooks and preparers. Together they can provide quality control for this fast-food operation.

4. Publicize the event in your church newsletter. Include a coupon for a free root beer with any order of fries and a hamburger.

5. Contact local merchants about donating food and paper items for the event.

Two weeks before the event.

1. Meet with members of the youth group to assign responsibilities, plan the menu and make preparations for all the '50s props necessary to create the atmosphere. (Guys can grease back their hair and wear black leather jackets. Girls can wear poodle skirts, bobby socks and tennis shoes. Other items you will need include a stereo, '50s records, bubble gum, nail aprons to keep change in, gas grills, order pads and all food supplies and paper products.)

2. Have carhops practice skating while they carry the trays with food orders on them. Train preparers to load the trays properly.

3. Publicize the event in your bulletin.

Two days before the event.

1. Organize a shopping crew with complete grocery lists, including accurate amounts for the expected crowd. Don't forget to purchase paper products and small packets of ketchup, salt, etc. Buy an excess of items. Running short will leave people with a negative feeling about the drive-in. Most leftover food could easily be purchased by families of youth group members and non-perishable items can be returned. (Save all sales receipts.)

2. Place lawn signs on the church lawn as public reminders. Make signs that give directions to the parking lot most accessible to your kitchen. Prepare directional signs for the parking

lot.

3. Check the church kitchen for adequate utensils. Borrow or purchase other items you will need.

4. Prepare order pads with the items you've included on your menu. Make sure you include prices and room for a total.

5. Go to the bank to get rolls of change for carhops to use.

Day of the event.

1. Ask the setup crew to arrive two hours before serving is to begin. Arrange the kitchen for food preparation. Set up the stereo and gas grills outside on the church lawn. Put up direction signs in the parking lot. Complete all food preparation that can be done in advance.

2. Ask other crews—carhops, cooks and quality-control people—to arrive one hour before the event. Give final instructions and make sure everyone knows his or her assigned task. Make sure carhops have adequate time to get into costume.

3. One-half hour before you "open," start the grills. Plan to have your first hamburgers coming off the grill as your first customers arrive. They will be impressed.

After the event.

1. Make sure church facilities—kitchen, lawn and parking lot—look better than when you arrived. Take down posters and signs around the church.

2. Do an accurate accounting of who assisted, and credit the accounts of those young people who helped raise funds.

3. Write thank-you notes to all the adult helpers and the people who made donations. Include a note of thanks in the church bulletin to all those who supported the young people by attending the 1950s Drive-In.

15 Ways to Avoid Concerns About Youth Group Fund Raising

Fund raising for events often brings criticisms and concern from some congregational members. Here are some helpful suggestions on how to avoid criticisms and respond to voiced concerns.

1. Keep your church staff, especially the senior minister, informed about your plans for the activity as well as the fund raisers to support it.

2. Go through the proper channels to receive approval for every project.

3. Provide information to church members to generate interest and encourage ownership in youth group activities.

4. Publicize positive accomplishments of young people in your church. For example, include reports on those who make the honor society, letter in a sport or receive a scholarship.

5. Help your young people choose activities that are not just "for fun," but also have service-related elements to them.

6. Encourage youth group members to give a percentage of the funds they raise to a service organization outside the church. (For example, when raising funds to take a trip to Mexico to work at an orphanage, raise 10 percent more to leave as a donation to buy food for the orphanage after you leave.)

7. Keep the number of fund-raising projects to a minimum. Don't have fund raisers unless you really need the funds.

8. Intersperse fund raisers with projects that don't raise money. Provide services to those who need them.

9. Solicit the help of your critics who have special skills and talents that could be utilized. They'll soon be on your side if they feel they are needed by you.

10. Give customers what they expect. Poor-quality products, items delivered late and impolite salespeople leave people with a bad feeling about any project.

11. Encourage church leaders to put youth group activities in the church budget. Some churches might choose to match funds being raised by the young people through their special projects.

12. Ask supportive parents and other adults in the congregation to make special gifts to your youth group program so that not as many fund raisers are needed. Developing a scholarship program for those with special needs is a great idea.

13. Publicly advertising your youth group's activities in the community is an excellent way to create positive feelings among church members.

14. Publicizing an event with pictures, a report in the worship service and obvious enthusiasm on the part of the young people will help church members feel good about supporting another youth event.

15. An appreciation dinner for the whole congregation, with personal invitations to those who made donations to the activity, is a great way of doing something special for those who made the activity a reality through their gifts. Make those individuals feel special and honored. Plan a program that shares the highlights of your activity.

A Final Word

Fund raising is a big task! Undertaking fund-raising projects with young people requires patience, planning, persistence and prayer. Don't neglect any of these. And remember, part of FUNd raising is FUN!

$ales

All-Church Bake-Off

The All-Church Bake-Off is a delicious fund raiser that can involve everyone in your congregation.

Encourage all church members to enter the bake-off by submitting baked goods in any of five categories—cakes, pies, cookies, candies and breads. First-place winners in each category receive trophies. Other top winners receive ribbons.

After the judging, auction the baked goods. By this time, the bake-off has attracted so much attention that auction attendance is great and bids are high.

Here are the rules for the bake-off:

● No age limit.

● Enter as many items as you wish in any or all of the five categories.

● Entries must be in by noon on the Sunday of the bake-off.

● Entries become the property of the youth group so that they can be sold at the auction.

Select judges from outside the church. Find caterers, bakers and other professionals. Have one for each category. Ask the judges to meet in the fellowship hall at 2 p.m. They score each entry—giving first consideration to taste. Appearance is secondary. After a top winner in each category is established, all judges taste these and vote on a grand-prize winner.

After the evening service that night, everyone converges on the fellowship hall for the announcement of winners and the giant auction. If you don't have a professional auctioneer in your congregation, use a good P.R. person to do the auctioneering.

Encourage everyone to enter the bake-off. It's not just the grandmas who have kitchen talents. The kids may surprise you.

To help promote the bake-off, encourage entrants to publicly challenge other people in the congregation. Publish people's challenges in the church bulletin—for example, "Mary Guest challenges Bob Galley." Those challenged do not have to accept, but the bulletin puts them on the spot, and they usually participate.

After the auction gather the prize-winning recipes and sell a special cookbook.

All-Night Bake Sale

Here's a bake sale with a different twist: an all-night baking party.

It is important to make items that you know most people enjoy such as chocolate chip and peanut butter cookies, brownies and hot fudge sauce. Use the church directory to call every member of the church and ask for orders. From the orders, calculate how much of each ingredient you need. Because of the size of your grocery order, the grocer may give you a reduced price.

Meet at the church early Friday evening and divide into various crews: mixers, bakers and packagers. Trade jobs throughout the entire night. Stop to have breakfast together and then deliver all the goodies.

After the cloud of flour settles, some members may never want to see another chocolate chip or peanut butter cookie. But it's a unifying experience to work together all night and make "dough" at the same time.

Auction Snacks

A steady year-round way to make money for your group is a refreshment service at auctions.

Contact a local auctioneer and express your willingness to provide refreshments at all of his or her auctions. Provide the table, coffeepots and other equipment. Keep the menu simple—coffee, Kool-Aid, doughnuts and hot dogs.

Ask the auctioneer to encourage the crowd to visit your stand. To run the stand, you'll need only three or four group members.

Box 'Em Up

If your church is near a college or university, this fund raiser is for you.

Every year at break time and the closing of classes for the summer, students face the problem of finding packing boxes while they pack and study for finals. Your group can sell boxes on campus as a service to the students and the youth

fund. Here's what to do.

Contact your local college or university, talk with the director of residential life and find out the school's break times. Explain your idea and ask for permission to sell boxes on campus.

Then get to work. Contact local businesses and ask them to save boxes for you. Some grocery stores save boxes for the general public, so you'll want to make periodic pickups. You'll need a storage area (someone's garage works fine) to keep and sort boxes according to size.

Three weeks before the break, go to the campus and get permission to hang posters that advertise your service. You could also send fliers about your sale to dorm residents through the on-campus mail service.

Arrange to have the use of a truck—or two trucks if you have lots of boxes. Make a big sign to call attention to your box sale; charge more for the large boxes than for the medium-size boxes.

Sale day should be about two weeks before the school's break. Go to a dorm parking lot and set up your big sign by the truck. Set sample boxes next to the sign. You'll need someone to collect boxes from inside the truck for your customers, someone to collect money, and others to help tote boxes to the dorms when bulk purchases are made.

And if your group is really ambitious, why not set up a lemonade stand?

Bread Festival

A Bread Festival mixes fun, fellowship and fund raising.

Ask all members (or their moms) to bake three loaves of their favorite kind of bread. Then, after church on Sunday, invite the congregation to the church kitchen or fellowship hall for the Bread Festival.

Serve free coffee and punch and allow everyone to taste samples of the different kinds of bread. Then encourage the samplers to buy loaves of their favorite breads. It's great fun, and since everyone likes homemade bread, you should sell out.

Business Directories

This fund raiser helps people get acquainted and learn what talents are available in the church. Publishing a business directory takes a lot of organization, but it's worth it.

First, get a list of all the people attending church. Contact each one in person or by mail to find out if he or she would make a contribution to be listed in a business directory. Publicize your directory in church bulletins and newsletters. Mail all members a letter with an order blank so people can respond immediately.

People don't have to be business people to be listed. Of course, you'll list them and the services they provide. But also list people with hobbies they can turn into services; for example, sewing, yard care, gardening and furniture refinishing. And don't forget children and teenagers. They can advertise for babysitting, pet sitting, lawn care and odd jobs. Establish a price scale for listings in the directory. Listings for business and professional services should cost the most, followed by home services and hobbies, and then kids' and teenagers' services.

When you have all the orders in, organize them according to various headings: business and professional services with subheads; home services and hobbies with subheads; and kids' corner with subheads.

Type the directory, make copies and staple the pages together. Give a copy of the directory to everyone who advertised in it. Then sell the directory to other church members.

When you're finished, youth group members will find a variety of job possibilities to explore.

Buy a Mile

This project is a takeoff on the old "rising thermometer" idea.

Take a large colored sheet of posterboard and sketch a map of your travel route to and from a destination such as the National Christian Youth Congress. Add up all of the travel expenses and divide by the total number of miles you will travel. After coming up with the cost per mile, begin drawing a red line over your route, showing how far you'll get on the money received thus far.

Give church members the opportunity over the next few months to help advance the group around the route by buying a number of miles. As you receive money each week, extend the line.

This plan has two primary benefits in addition to the money raised. First, it unifies the church family in supporting the youth group. The whole project is one of cooperation because church contributions are combined with funds raised in other ways. Second, the chart provides a great visual picture of how the group is doing. It becomes a focal point each Sunday as group members and the congregation come to church.

Chili-Making Fun

This activity is sure to warm up the wintertime and add

spice to any youth group.

Have a chili-making contest and fund raiser. Challenge your group members and other church members to compete against one another in pursuit of the best-tasting chili.

Publicize the contest/fund raiser well in advance. Generate excitement and interest. Have competitors fill out entry forms and state how much chili they will make. Also have purchasers place orders that specify how much chili they plan to buy. Make sure you will have enough; plan on more than you have orders for.

Hold the contest/sale on a Saturday afternoon in the church or in a member's home.

First, the contest: Ask your pastor and a few other church officers to be the judges. Line up samples of the entries in numbered bowls. Provide glasses of water, spoons, bibs and voting cards. When the judges make their selection, award your winner with a large chili bowl, scoop and a bottle of mouthwash.

Then, the sale: Fill small, medium and large containers with the chili and determine prices for the different amounts. Sell away!

This can be lots of fun. Try it!

Cider Sells

Here's an idea for your group to do during the autumn months.

Post a request on the church bulletin board asking people to donate apples or to allow you to pick apples in their yards or orchards.

Find a church member or friend who has an apple grinder and a cider press. Ask people to donate bottles for the cider. Then the only expense for this project is time and labor.

Once you gather the apples, have your group members form an assembly line. You'll want to sort and wash the apples; wash the bottles; grind the apples; press the apple pulp; strain the apple juice; and bottle the fresh cider.

This activity involves everyone and there's always plenty to do. It provides for a great time of fellowship because everyone works toward a common goal. You'll be able to make dozens of gallons of cider during one evening.

For added fun, let a few kids dress like Johnny Appleseed when they sell the cider. Have some of the church women donate apple pies, and sell them by the slice.

This idea may sound like hard work, but the profit is worth it!

Cinnamon Roll Sale

Your local public school system most likely serves great cinnamon rolls. For a fund raiser, hire a local school's cooks to bake cinnamon rolls for your group to sell.

Take orders a few days before the cooks go to work. Most people love cinnamon rolls, so you'll be able to pay your cooks generously and still make a healthy profit.

Collective Auction

Raise funds in a fun and lucrative way. First, receive contributions of objects (books, records, cassette tapes). Then auction each item, but not in the usual way.

A judge sets an alarm to go off at an unknown, prearranged time (one minute, 30 seconds, two minutes or whatever). All may bid as much as they want, regardless of how much was previously bid. When the alarm goes off, the item goes to the last bidder. Now, *all* bids are collected.

For example, Fred bids, "One dollar!" Janet bids, "Two fifty!" Harold bids, "Two dollars!" Ring! Harold wins the item and $5.50 is collected.

College Cookie Factory

Capitalize on people's basic love of home-baked chocolate chip cookies and make a fortune, especially if your church is near a college or university.

Send letters and order forms to nearby colleges and parents clubs around the country (addresses provided by the college) and explain your program, offering to deliver cookies to the parents' sons and daughters on dates selected to correspond with exam periods at the college. Allow room on each order form for a message to the receiver of the cookies.

As the orders pile in, organize for action: bakers, wrappers, bag logo designers and artists, gift tag writers and deliverers. Schedule each production for a Friday evening and Saturday morning.

For added profits, sell cookies after each of the college's home football games. Here's an example of an order form:

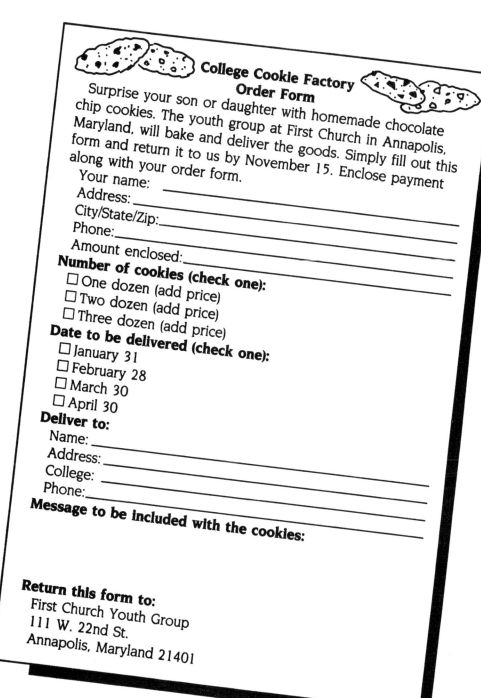

College Cookie Factory Order Form

Surprise your son or daughter with homemade chocolate chip cookies. The youth group at First Church in Annapolis, Maryland, will bake and deliver the goods. Simply fill out this form and return it to us by November 15. Enclose payment along with your order form.

Your name: _____

Address: _____

City/State/Zip: _____

Phone: _____

Amount enclosed: _____

Number of cookies (check one):
☐ One dozen (add price)
☐ Two dozen (add price)
☐ Three dozen (add price)

Date to be delivered (check one):
☐ January 31
☐ February 28
☐ March 30
☐ April 30

Deliver to:
Name: _____
Address: _____
College: _____
Phone: _____

Message to be included with the cookies: _____

Return this form to:
First Church Youth Group
111 W. 22nd St.
Annapolis, Maryland 21401

Cookie Walk

If you're looking for a delicious way to raise funds, you might try a Cookie Walk. Bake a variety of cookies (the more the better) and raise money by selling cardboard "cookie boxes" to church members and others in the community. The size of the box and price are up to you.

During the Cookie Walk, those who've bought boxes walk around tables laden with dozens of cookies, choosing their own assortment.

Because this differs from a regular bake sale, be sure to include a short description of what a Cookie Walk is all about when you announce the date and time of your event.

And remember that you can sell cookie boxes several days or even weeks before the actual affair. In addition to giving you time to reach more people, selling boxes before the date of the Cookie Walk will give you an indication of how many cookies your group should bake.

Creative Calendars

Creative Calendars help church members think of their youth group throughout the year. This unique idea draws your group closer together and helps it earn money too!

You'll need a camera; sheets of 8½×11 plain white paper; 10 ½-inch small, plastic spiral binders; ready-made, 8½×11 monthly calendar sheets (obtain these at any office supply store or drugstore); black markers; large cardboard box panels (refrigerator-size); scissors or knives; white tempera paint; a spiral-hole punch; and a single-hole punch.

First, have kids draw and cut out large numbers (each at least 5 feet tall) of the coming year using scissors or knives and the cardboard panels. Paint each number with white tempera paint.

Second, arrange a day for everyone to dress up for a group picture. Have several kids stand up the numbers and hold them. Have the rest of the young people sit in front of the numbers. The teenagers holding the numbers can look around them, peer through holes, or just stand beside them. Take a picture of the group. (The picture can be black and white to save expense.) Enlarge the picture to 8½×11 inches and reproduce it onto heavy white paper. The picture becomes the calendar cover.

Third, divide kids into even-numbered groups. Assign a certain month (or months) to each group. Members in each group must design a picture for their assigned month (or months) using the black markers and the 8½×11 plain white paper. Tell them to create a theme for the picture they draw. For instance, draw a big heart with an arrow through it for the month of February, the sweetheart month. Type or print one scripture verse on each month's calendar sheet.

Finally, list each group member's birthday and coming year's youth events on a separate page. Place this page after the month of December.

Make as many copies of the calendar as you desire before assembling it. Use the spiral-hole punch to punch the top of each calendar page. Then assemble the calendar months in order (make sure the artwork for each month is at the top and the calendar month on the bottom when the calendar's open to hang on the wall). Insert the plastic spiral binder on each calendar. Use the single-hole punch to punch a hole in the middle of the bottom of each page for easy hanging.

Your group will learn the importance of teamwork and earn money at the same time.

Dime-a-Dip Dinner

Want to change the standard boring fellowship dinner into a simple fund raiser? How about a Dime-a-Dip Dinner?

Two weeks prior to the event, have group members call members of the congregation and ask them to bring various meats, vegetables, salads and desserts for the "dip" dinner.

At the dinner itself, people pay a dime per dip of food that they choose. They'll be surprised and delighted when they receive a super meal for a small cost. It's an easy way to earn money.

Make sure the dinner is well-publicized and provide some entertainment.

Doughnut Deliveries

Deliver doughnuts on weekends as a service to the church and community—and your youth budget. Here's how you do it.

Group members take orders for freshly baked doughnuts from their families, friends, neighbors, etc. The price per dozen of doughnuts includes delivery between 8 and 9 on Saturday morning. A baker in town gets up early to make the doughnuts (you may have an all-night doughnut shop where you could buy them). One young person picks up the doughnuts and takes them to the church where the rest of the members collect them for delivery to the homes.

Fertilizer Sale

Need a good springtime fund raiser? Sell fertilizer! It's one of those products many people need to buy, and they might as well help green their lawns and your group's treasury at the same time.

Publicize your fertilizer sale and take orders at church for several Sundays. Spend a couple of Saturdays selling door to door. Give careful information to group members about the fertilizer's chemical content so they can answer any questions.

After collecting all the orders, buy 50-pound bags of fertilizer from a local fertilizer company. Have the company deliver the stuff to the church on a designated Saturday. Customers then come and present their receipts to claim their fertilizer.

Fireplace Fire Starters

Fireplace owners will appreciate this: Your group can make and sell attractive fireplace fire starters.

You'll need a paper cutter, kitchen tongs, cardboard boxes, shoe boxes, scrap cloths, ribbon, markers, scissors, glue, tape, 9×9 old baking pans, half-or-more-burned candles, an outside grill, charcoal, lighter fluid and matches. Put a notice in your church newsletter and bulletin to solicit items you need.

When all is ready, find a spot on someone's patio or back yard and set up shop. One person uses the paper cutter and cuts the cardboard boxes into 4-inch squares. Another person tends the grill and, as necessary, puts candles into the baking pans to produce the wax. The next person uses the kitchen tongs to dip the cardboard squares into the heated wax and then sets the wax-coated squares on cardboard (not yet cut) for drying. Some group members decorate the shoe boxes with the scrap cloth pieces, ribbon and markers. And finally, others count 50 cooled fire starters and neatly pack them into each decorated shoe box.

Working right along, your group can produce 400 to 600

fireplace fire starters per hour. It takes a bit longer to finish packing them attractively.

Depending on the amount of tinder and kindling in a fireplace, it takes only one or two fire starters to get a great fire going. They ignite with a single match and burn completely, leaving no wax residue in the fireplace.

Choose a cold Sunday morning and sell your fire starters after the worship service; business will never be better.

For-Your-Good-Health Dinner

Raise much-needed cash and provide healthy food with a For-Your-Good-Health Dinner.

Serve only food recommended by health organizations. The American Cancer Society, the American Heart Association, health-food stores or diet organizations will be glad to provide menus and recipes.

Have a qualified medical person weigh and give a blood-pressure test to each guest before dinner. Distribute weight and blood-pressure pamphlets. Charge parents and friends a small fee to sample the food.

Who knows? You might even convert someone to eating healthy foods.

Fruit Kabobs Sale

Bake sales are great fund raisers. People seem to enjoy them—except for weight watchers. So, why not hold a Fruit Kabobs Sale as an alternative to brownies and cake? Buy a watermelon, three honeydew melons, two pineapples and a few mangoes.

Before the Sunday evening service, gather in the church kitchen. Some group members cut the fruit into chunks and others spear a chunk of each fruit onto wooden fondue sticks. Make several dozen of these fruit treats, lay them on trays

and put them into the refrigerator. Following the benediction, pull the trays out of the refrigerator. Serve the kabobs with punch and coffee.

Weight watchers aren't the only ones who appreciate the kabobs. Even heavy eaters like the variety of fresh fruit.

The Great Salad Bar Experience

This profitable fund raiser is easy to coordinate. Here's how it works.

Several weeks before the event, make a sign-up sheet for

group members to choose which salad bar items to bring. Include soups, bread, Jell-O, toppings, dressings, lettuce, paper plates, cups, etc., and suggested amounts.

Announce the event and ask adults to also sign up to contribute some of the salad bar items on the list. If needed, you can buy extra items at reduced prices if you explain the fund raiser to grocery-store managers.

Write reminders for those who have signed up to bring their items before the morning worship service on the designated day. Ask some of the teenagers to help you set up the salad bar and wait on "customers" after the service. Choose one group member to collect the set fee or donations.

Homemade Take-Home TV Dinner Sale

Here is an idea for your group to raise funds and provide meals for people in the congregation who want to watch a Sunday televised event (such as a football game). Begin the sale at noon, just as the morning worship service is concluding.

Group members prepare casserole dishes and package them in disposable containers (with salad and dessert). Then they sell them in a high visibility area to folks as they leave for home after worship.

During the Sunday prior to the sale, announce the upcoming fund raiser, emphasizing that the dinners will help the youth group while lifting some of the pressures facing the church members. (Members won't have to worry about going out to eat, can get home to watch most of the game, and won't need to prepare something before coming to church.) Also publicize the sale in the morning bulletin and the church newsletter. "Fill your stomachs and fund the fun-loving young people of the church" is a good slogan.

Sell the dinners at a minimum price, but allow for generous donations in order not to undersell your product.

Hot Potato Sale

With the opening of restaurants with baked potato specialties, your group can cash in by hosting a potato feast for the congregation after Sunday worship.

The Saturday before the luncheon, meet at the church kitchen to bake the potatoes and prepare salads and toppings for the potatoes. Offer toppings such as butter, sour cream, cheese, bacon bits and chili.

On Sunday morning, heat the potatoes during worship. After the benediction quickly set up for the potato feast. Charge a fee for a potato, salad and drink. Also sell homemade baked goods. You'll raise money and provide the congregation a nutritious and light meal.

Light Bulb Sale

Light bulbs make a good fund raiser. Here's how to do it.

Locate a wholesale light bulb dealer in town. You may need to make some phone calls to find a wholesaler. (One company that sells wholesale bulbs for fund raising is United Fund Raisers Co., Box 894, Dothan, AL 36302, 1-800-633-7557.)

Sell the bulbs for a few cents lower than what is marked on the packs. You should make a good profit because the wholesale cost is about half the marked price.

Buy the bulbs in this ratio: two 60-watt; one 75-watt; and two 100-watt. This is a good indicator of the way people buy bulbs.

Require members to sell 50 packs. Allow members to keep half the profit on every pack over the first 50 they sell.

Lunches to Go

Most people plan to do something after church or are hungry immediately following the service. Making Sunday lunch a convenience is a temptation hardly anyone can refuse. Brown paper bags and simple foods make this activity easy and fun as well as a positive service to the people in your congregation.

Start by choosing simple lunch items: sandwiches, fruit, milk or juice, brownies or cookies, napkins and plastic silverware. You may also want to include a surprise snack such as scripture cards taped to a Hershey's Kiss. You might want to have kids write scripture passages on pieces of paper to insert with the lunch. Using markers, decorate the lunch sacks with designs. Advertise them as "designer lunches." Set up a table in the foyer. Drape it in a tablecloth and decorate with crepe paper. Have signs that say "Lunches to Go." Teenage servers wear aprons or chefs' hats.

Prepare the lunches before the church service. Don't set a price for the lunches but allow people to offer donations. Have someone give an announcement in the morning service about the Lunches to Go fund raiser. Take photos during the fund raiser. Make a poster a week after the event with the pictures and total amount raised. Put it up on a church bulletin board.

Use this idea once a year; perhaps more often. Summer is an excellent time of the year for Lunches to Go, when people are involved in outdoor activities and may not have enough time to fix their own lunch.

Make Money With Manufacturers' Refunds

Here's an idea to help finance your group's next project.

Manufacturers pay money for the proofs of purchase on specified products. Save boxes, labels, containers, lids and receipts.

Then make an orderly refunding bank. Use these two categories: food (edible items); and non-food (non-edible items). Use a large box, envelope or plastic bag for files.

Obtain refund forms from grocery stores, drugstores and auto centers. These forms are small printed pieces of paper that say something such as "One dollar back for four UPCs from our product." (UPCs, or Universal Pricing Codes, are the bars and numbers on products signaling their prices.)

Check store bulletin boards and aisles each week for refund forms. Most stores don't limit the number of forms you take, but only take as many as you can use.

Gather forms and file them in a small box according to their expiration dates.

Each person takes one of the different forms and collects the correct number of items from the refunding bank. Each member fills out the form with his or her own name, home address, and then mails it. Most offers limit one per person, address or household, so read the fine print.

Have fun raising money.

Pie Social and Face Auction

To raise funds for your ever-empty youth coffer, hold a Pie Social and Face Auction.

Designate five youth group members to get 35 to 40 individuals to each bake or buy and donate one pie. The pies are to be used for the social scheduled after a Sunday evening worship service.

Then ask all the board members and deacons to donate their faces for the face auction to be held during the pie social. Require the youth pastor and senior pastor to be involved in the fun too.

The youth group purchases Styrofoam cups, paper plates, plastic forks, Dixie cups, ice cream, coffee, whipping cream and pie tins. Group members prepare whipped cream pies for the face auction.

For a fee, each person receives a slice of the pie of his or her choice, coffee and a Dixie cup filled with ice cream.

Ask an auctioneer, chosen from the congregation, to drive up the prices of the faces. The highest bidder gets to throw a whipped cream pie at the face purchased.

This fund raiser is a big hit.

Popping for Profit

With a few donations and minimum effort, popcorn can puff up huge profits for your youth group.

If some parents are critical of popcorn as junk food, just ask, "What is more natural than corn?" If you use a hot-air popper and no salt or butter, all those crispy little fluffs in that 4-cup bag add up to about 100 calories.

Borrow two or three electric poppers, and ask people to donate butter-flavored salt, small paper sacks and lots of popcorn.

Obtain permission from a school principal to sell popcorn on the campus every day after school for a week (or every Friday for a month).

Ask for volunteers to publicize the event at the school. Arrange a regular time and place to pop popcorn and bag the goods. Then set up a rotating schedule to be sure everyone gets a chance to be involved.

Go ahead and try this fund-raising project. You'll have a lot of fun while you produce 100 percent profit.

Sundae Sunday

Put on an ice cream smorgasbord and entertainment for the people in your church.

Buy a large quantity of vanilla ice cream (7 gallons feeds 100 people). Sell dishes of ice cream.

Set up a table with all kinds of ice cream toppings so the people can visit this table and create their own sundaes. Toppings include hot fudge, hot butterscotch, hot caramel, strawberries, marshmallow cream, brandied fruit, chopped nuts, sprinkles, granola, coconut and whipped cream. (It is best to have these donated because the expense of buying commercial toppings is prohibitive.)

Jobs for group members include scoopers, runners who keep topping supplies filled, table managers who help children serve toppings, people who serve the whipped cream (less waste to have someone serve it), people who take money and tickets, and people who clean up.

There are many options for entertainment. The youth choir could do a concert; members could perform a talent show; or a group could do a musical.

Sell tickets in advance. Plan for more people than the tickets you sell. Some people may buy two dishes of ice cream during the event.

A couple of helpful hints: Check with local dairies to see about their bulk pack ice cream prices and/or keep your eyes open for sales at local grocery stores. Fondue pots are great for serving hot toppings.

Twinkie Tradin'

This fund raiser is pleasantly fun and successful.

Divide your group into teams of about four people. Each team receives a Twinkie (or some other item of similar value) along with pencil and paper. Team members then go door to door and barter with residents in the neighborhood. (To barter is to agree to a simple exchange of items; no money is involved.)

Each team tries to make as many trades as possible, with the objective to end up with something of greater value. When kids explain their purpose, most neighbors are willing to help.

Have teams record on paper all trades made. For instance, Twinkie traded for can of pop; can of pop traded for comic book; and comic book traded for '55 Chevy convertible.

When the group gathers back at your meeting place, give prizes to the teams with the following:

● The most trades.
● The most valuable item.
● The funniest anecdote from the bartering sessions.

If your group is large or your barter items are expensive, auction the items at a church event.

Vintage T-Shirt Auction

T-shirts get better with age. Why not capitalize on that and bring in some youth group funds?

If you print special T-shirts for retreats, camps or special events, you probably have a pile of vintage T-shirts stuck in a closet. And so do other church members. Those T-shirts deserve better than becoming dust rags.

Collect them for a Vintage T-Shirt Auction.

Advertise an auction with T-shirts dating back to the earliest year you have a shirt for. Get as many people to donate

shirts as you can.

Start the bidding any way you like. Highlight the special events and places the T-shirts commemorate. Watch the fun as kids and adults buy replacements for their favorite shirts.

Youth Group Stockholders

If you're going on a mission trip or if you need to raise money for another project, invite adults (18 or older) to invest in the youth group by becoming stockholders.

This simple idea generates enthusiasm among adults—and money in the youth fund.

Get a plain stock certificate from a stockbroker in town. Copy the format and adapt the language to suit your own purposes.

Publicize this opportunity for six weeks and sell stock at a set amount per share. (Solicit involvement from non-church adults by running a news release in your local newspaper, telling why you're raising the money.) All stockholders receive official-looking certificates that document their support.

Upon completion of your project, send all the stockholders invitations (with R.S.V.P.s) to a banquet run by the youth group. Each share is worth one free admission. Show slides, talk about the experiences and give your supporters a special thank-you.

You'll net a good profit after the banquet.

$ervices

1950s Drive-In

Turn your church parking lot into a drive-in scene from the 1950s and make money while you have fun.

Post on the building a large menu that offers hamburgers, hot dogs, french fries, coffee, soda pop and ice cream. Bubble-gum-chewing, roller-skating carhops take orders and skate trays of food to customers. Prepare all of the food on gas grills at a large work area facing the cars. Everyone dresses in the 1950s theme: leather jackets, bobby socks and greased hair. The customers enjoy watching the members work and laugh together. Free pieces of bubble gum come with each order. Music from the 1950s blares into the parking lot.

Open the drive-in from 5 to 7:30 p.m. on a Saturday. Expenses include hamburgers, hot dogs, french fries, cooking oil, coffee, soda pop, ketchup, mustard, relish, onions, bubble gum, napkins, order pads, pens, paper cups for ice cream, plastic spoons and skate rental.

Fast-food restaurants may donate several of these items, and some stores may offer church discounts. For example, ask your local baker if your cooking crew can borrow some aprons. Ask a lumber dealer to give nail aprons for the carhops to keep change. Borrow gas grills from church members.

Publicize the drive-in with posters, fliers and press releases.

You'll earn a good profit, have a lot of fun and relive the nostalgic days of the 1950s era drive-ins.

Business Carwash

A new twist in carwashes: Plan a carwash to service business people and companies.

Set your date for a Friday (during a school vacation or day off) and choose an available parking lot in the central part of the city. Earlier in the week, visit businesses and make appointments to pick up employee and company cars during office hours to wash and clean the autos. (Check your church insurance policy to see if it covers damage to cars.)

Also check the Yellow Pages for locations of any industrial parks or companies that would have lots of company cars (for example, cab companies or truck and bus firms).

Working people appreciate this convenience; they don't have to spend weekend time getting their cars washed.

If you take donations only, you'll make plenty of money. If possible, plan this once a month and build your clientele.

Another twist in carwashes is to plan a "free" carwash. Don't charge people to wash their cars. Instead, solicit sponsors who pledge a certain amount of money for each car washed. Publicize the carwash in the church and surrounding area so people will bring their cars. Then wash as many cars as possible in the time you have.

Cafe Takeover

"Take over" a local restaurant.

Make arrangements with a local restaurant to work on a given Saturday as waiters and waitresses, cashiers, and hosts and hostesses. The management agrees to pay a percentage of the profits for the day to the group.

Involve group members in a day of training and orientation prior to the workday.

Do extensive publicity with posters, fliers and announcements in the church paper to encourage people to eat at the restaurant during that day. This is great free publicity for the restaurant.

No costs are involved. And in addition to making big money, a Cafe Takeover is a great experience for the group.

For added income, plan a carwash simultaneously in the restaurant's parking lot.

Church Cleaning

Many small churches use volunteer janitors for weekly cleaning and other maintenance tasks. This fund raiser provides an opportunity to perform a needed service and also raise money.

After receiving permission from the appropriate church board, divide the youth group into teams. The teams will rotate cleaning each week. Teams should be large enough to clean the church in a reasonable amount of time, but there should be enough teams so no team cleans more than once or twice a month. Place one adult volunteer on each team and find a coordinator for the whole project.

The church should furnish supplies. But it will count on the kids' dependability to get the church to sparkle each week.

You can take on projects throughout the year—and earn clean money.

Dog Wash

Raise money for the local Humane Society with a Dog Wash.

Charge a few cents per pound for each dog you wash. Weigh the dogs on a regular bathroom scale and then carry them over to the wash crews. Soap, scrub and then rinse the dogs with a garden hose. Dry the dogs with old rags and a blow-dryer.

Hold the Dog Wash on the church's parking lot on a Saturday. Since the proceeds go toward a good cause, newspapers may help publicize the event. Some dog owners may be so pleased with the results that they promise additional donations to the Humane Society.

You'll need soap, water, a bathroom scale, a garden hose, blow-dryers, old rags, old brushes and an energetic crew.

Flag Painters

Earn money by painting little red mailbox flags.

Group members go door to door in their neighborhoods, charging homeowners a small fee to paint the little flags.

Materials required are red enamel paint, some small cups for paint, and paintbrushes for each member.

Gutting Buildings

Your group can earn lots of money by gutting old houses and buildings.

Banks are always foreclosing or buying old houses that need repair and renovation. Contractors often shy away from gutting buildings. They are far more interested in buying buildings that are ready for plumbers, electricians and carpenters to begin work immediately.

First, meet with bank officials. Explain that your group is interested in providing a community-oriented service to earn funds. The group provides the tools, safety gear (hard hats, safety goggles, etc.), insurance and experienced adult supervision. The bank pays the group for the service, the sum depending on the going rate for gutting buildings.

Undertake a small house as your first project. You'll love ripping out old paint-covered wallboard, wood lath, ceilings and windows. Arrange to have pickups or dump trucks haul the debris to the nearest dump.

Depending on the dimensions of the building, your group can earn hundreds of dollars for one or two days of work. You'll learn helpful skills, provide a useful service to your community and have lots of fun.

Help-a-Thon

Raise some cash and become aware of the needs in your community. Set aside a Saturday in the fall to work on the homes and yards of the elderly and handicapped in your community. Help them ready their homes for the cold months ahead.

For each hour of work, raise pledges from family, church members and friends at school. Most people are eager to support this effort to help the elderly and handicapped.

Working for the elderly and handicapped will give you a deep sense of satisfaction; most people are happy simply to have someone talk with them. And a lot of important work gets done. You'll remember this experience for a long time.

Help Them Give

Here's a fund raiser that provides a needed service to rest home residents.

Check with the rest home ahead of time to get permission to hold a Christmas gift bazaar. Get any special guidelines or suggestions. Also find out the best time to visit and whether it's okay to hang posters announcing your bazaar.

Gather the gifts: Request donations from church families. Make some craft items. Create Christmas decorations and cards; be creative. Have a variety of gifts and cards to offer.

Take your group and its wares to the rest home. Enjoy the visit! Talk with the residents and share the spirit of Christmas with them.

Keep prices low enough to be affordable, and offer tag-writing and gift-wrapping services. Also provide free delivery of gifts to local families.

Remember to sing Christmas carols to the residents before you deliver the gifts.

Hugs for H.O.P.E.

How often have you seen the bumper sticker that says, "Have you hugged your kid today?" Kids aren't the only ones who deserve a hug every day. This fund raiser allows worshipers to receive hugs from youth group members in exchange for contributions. Everyone seems to love the idea.

Announce your fund-raising idea near Valentine's Day or when your pastor preaches a sermon on love, hunger or missions. Actually, any Sunday is appropriate. You might want to earmark proceeds for a special fund to help the needy of your church or community. You could call this special fund H.O.P.E.: Help Our People in Emergency.

After setting a date for your fund raiser, buy posterboard and marking pens. Have kids design announcements emphasizing what H.O.P.E. is and how you'll use the proceeds. Hang the posters around the church. Encourage each "hugger" to make his or her own contribution box.

You may want to make hug coupons that people purchase and keep to get hugs throughout the year. These coupons entitle the owner to a hug from any group member. Make hug coupons from 3x5 index cards using the following words: "The bearer of this coupon is entitled to one hug from any youth group member at any time throughout the year." You may want to draw a heart with the words "Hugs for H.O.P.E." printed on it. You could also write scriptures about love on the cards.

Announce the fund raiser during worship and set a time limit for the hugging. Have the kids go around to congregration members soliciting hugs and selling hug coupons.

Hugs for H.O.P.E. is a great self-esteem builder for everyone. Besides, everyone benefits from a hug.

Hunger Kidnap

Kidnap your minister and help fight world hunger.

Kidnap your pastor on a Saturday night and hold him or her for ransom. While the pastor is tied and blindfolded, group members call each family in the congregation. Request a ransom of money and/or canned goods to be brought to church the next morning to help fight hunger.

After you place all the calls, set your pastor free. Then have a lock-in and study the problems of world hunger. Prepare a worship service for the following morning.

Send the money you collect to a hunger-fighting organization such as one of the following:

● Christian Children's Fund, Inc., Box 26511, Richmond, VA 23261.

● Compassion International, Box 7000, Colorado Springs, CO 80933.

● Food for the Hungry, Inc., Box E, Scottsdale, AZ 85252.

● World Vision, 919 W. Huntington Dr., Monrovia, CA 91016.

Give the canned goods to needy families in your area.

Hunger Scavenger Hunt

Item	Points
Powdered milk	1 pt. per lb.
Turkey (whole, frozen)	5 pts. per lb.
Ham (canned)	4 pts. per lb.
Rice	2 pts. per lb.
Beans (dry)	2 pts. per lb.
Sugar	2 pts. per lb.
Flour	2 pts. per lb.
Macaroni or spaghetti	1 pt. per lb.
Noodles	1 pt. per lb.
Canned vegetables	1 pt. per can
Peanut butter	4 pts. per jar
Cake/cookie/brownie mix	2 pts. per box
Canned fruit	1 pt. per can
Vitamins (multi-type)	3 pts. per 100
Soup (cans or mixes)	2 pts. each
Cooking oil	3 pts. per bottle
Shortening (Crisco-type)	3 pts. per can
Canned meat (tuna, corned beef, etc.)	3 pts. per can
Jell-o/pudding (cans or boxed)	1 pt. each
$ Money $ (to purchase food)	1 pt. per $1.00
(Other items will be judged accordingly)	

Instead of the usual "Let's collect canned goods for the poor," add a new twist.

Call a local food distribution center and explain the project. Set a day three weeks away for your group to deliver the collected food.

Announce the beginning of the Hunger Scavenger Hunt (have some enthusiastic group members help) and hand out the list of items to be found. The list should also include the number of points per pound, can, box or dollar that will be awarded.

Pair off group members and challenge them to contact grocery stores, neighbors and church members. They should explain what they're doing and ask for vitamins, canned goods, money, frozen turkeys, ham or other meats.

On the designated day, pairs bring their collected food items to the church. Tally the points for every pound, can or dollar collected. Give a surprise gift—a frozen chicken—to the pair with the most points.

Gather the items in a truck and deliver them to the center. Kids will have fun and want to do this project again.

Junk Metal Collection

Collect scrap metal and make a profit.

Find out who your local scrap metal dealers are. Then start collecting everything containing metal: water heaters, motors, refrigerators, car parts, aluminum cans, pipes, you name it. Tell the congregation members that you'll pick up any junk metal they have. Also look along roads and in old dumping sites. Stop at homes and businesses where you see scrap lying around. Most people are eager to get rid of the junk.

After you have a full load, return to the church and disassemble it all, separating the metals. You might also collect lead, car batteries and insulated wire. You will need only a couple of complete toolboxes, several magnets and a vehicle. You might want to borrow someone's flatbed truck.

You'll have great fun taking all those furnaces, lawn mowers and appliances apart. Your group will also feel good about cleaning up the community and recycling non-renewable resources.

Live Mannequins

Become "live dummies" at a local department store.

Work through the promotion director of the store. Group members select two or three outfits of clothing from the

racks. On a rotating basis, the young people pose as manne-
quins in four or five staging areas, including the display
windows. They are not allowed to move for a period of 10 to
15 minutes. Once a model moves, smiles or laughs, the
modeling session at that area is over. It's quite a challenge to
keep a straight face when your friends stand outside the windows and make faces!

The store probably won't give the group any money. The
store's contribution is providing the clothing and the modeling
areas. The group members raise money by soliciting pledges
for each minute they actually pose in immobile positions.
They pose two or three times, wearing a different outfit each
time. Even at a few cents per minute, the money adds up.

The store can receive a great deal of attention—from customers and the media—with this project. So, many stores may
be willing to pay your group a set amount.

Kids have a great time. Customers actually come up to them
without realizing they're alive. They finger and discuss the
clothing. When they finally realize the "mannequin" is alive,
everyone will roar with laughter.

Mission Marathon

Marathons often bring in big bucks but too often fail to accomplish anything of real significance. A Mission Marathon
could be the answer.

Group members find sponsors for every hour spent at the

marathon (24 hours). The marathon includes a variety of worthwhile projects and learning activities that focus on missions.

Invite speakers from various youth missionary movements to share their organizations' goals and ministries. Show films on missionary efforts in hungry lands, the inner cities and your own community.

Most important, work on several projects to help missionaries. Package bars of soap for missionaries. (Soap is greatly appreciated at many mission stations.) For medical missionaries, you can roll bandages from strips of used bed sheets. Ask hotels and congregation members to donate the sheets. Group members can also canvass the neighborhood for cans and packages of food to give to local food banks.

This fund raiser will give a great boost to the morale of your group members.

Parents Day Off

Renew youth group funds with this old idea: sitting for children on a Saturday.

First, plan a strategy: games, soccer, softball, bike riding, coloring and craft projects, etc., all based at the church. Soup and sandwiches are the perfect lunch (especially with lots of peanut butter and jelly).

Then publicize your services and establish a fee for each category: one child, all day (9 to 5), lunch included; one child, half day (9 to 1), lunch included; two or three children, all day, lunch included; two or three children, half day, lunch included; four or five children, all day, lunch included; and four or five children, half day, lunch included.

Parents drop off their kids at 9 a.m. and pay when they pick them up. They love this service! Some parents clean the house, go on day trips, visit special friends or just spend some time alone.

Note: While this fund raiser is always *timely* (ask any parent), some *times* may be more productive for your youth fund such as Christmas shopping season or Mother's and Father's Day weekends. Or—you might consider providing this service once a month!

Pennies Make Sense

Men battle women in a race to collect and contribute the most pennies for the youth fund.

Set up a large, old-fashioned wooden scale with copper buckets in the church lobby. The men are to load one bucket with pennies; the women, the other. The contest lasts eight weeks, and each Sunday group members empty the buckets,

count the pennies and prepare the next week's bulletin insert, which announces the accumulated results and also keeps up interest and enthusiasm.

Some people may want to contribute but only have silver and bills. That's okay—just exchange those at a bank. That way, at the end of the contest, you can line up the pennies side by side and try to win a spot in the *Guinness Book of World Records*.

Group members spend an evening wrapping the pennies. The fun part is taking the wrapped coins to the bank.

Photographing Pets for Profit

For fun and funds, your youth group can run a pet portrait service! Many people consider pets "part of the family," but few portrait studios photograph pets.

Advertise your service in church newsletters, in school news-

papers and on community bulletin boards. Once you get started, word of mouth will keep customers coming to you.

Use a 35mm single-lens reflex camera. Use color slide film and let the owner choose which transparency he or she wants printed. If black-and-white film is preferred, have a "contact sheet" made and let the owner choose from that.

Some tips: Carry a wire grooming brush for last-minute pet touch-ups. Get acquainted with the pet first, and have the owner present. Choose familiar-to-the-pet surroundings and an uncluttered background. A light-colored animal looks best against a dark-colored background, and vice versa. Avoid shadows. Use a pet's favorite toy to divert its attention. (Don't use an edible toy unless you know the pet is trained to sit or beg before receiving a treat.) Photograph the pet in a variety of poses.

Set your fee for each customer according to the cost of film and developing, and add a percentage of that amount for your profit.

And hope it rains cats and dogs!

Radio Day

Have a Radio Day on one of your local radio stations.

Work out a suitable day with the station management. February is a slow period of the year for some stations. Organize a sales committee of young people and adults who call on businesses to encourage them to advertise during Radio Day. The station establishes the rates. Split the advertising income 50-50 with the station.

Members read the ads live on Radio Day. Use creative techniques such as skits, choral ads and so on.

Radio Day not only raises money for your group, but it

gives your group and church some positive exposure to the radio audience.

Rock Concert

Get your group together this spring and throw some rocks. And get paid for it.

Clear farmers' fields of stones before the spring planting. The farmers will appreciate the service. They're happy to pay

because the rock-clearing service saves them the expense of repairing rock-damaged machinery later in the season.

The farmers furnish the tractor, wagon and driver. They pay either by the acre or by the total hours worked.

The fellowship and exercise are great, especially while unloading the rocks. All the noise produced by the rocks hitting each other inspires the nickname for this fund raiser—Rock Concert.

Small Amounts Count

Here is an easy, profitable fund raiser. Remind your youth group that if every member gives a little, it helps the total a lot.

Give each group member a plastic dime container. Most coin or hobby stores sell the inexpensive containers. Ask your young people to contribute a certain number of dimes a day for 20 days for whatever project you choose. When the containers are collected, emptied and the dimes counted, the money will make a significant contribution to your project.

Also ask the congregation members to join you. Again, emphasize that when everyone pitches in, a lot can be accomplished.

Tin Can Fortune

This project will serve your community and raise funds for your youth group. It's fun too.

Get pledges for each discarded can or bottle you can collect. Then when the big day arrives, give group members trash bags and send them out in pairs to hit the roadsides, parks, schoolyards and any other places such litter might be found. You might also go door to door to request cans or bottles.

Kids meet back at the church or someone's house at an

appointed time to sort the cans and bottles, tally the amount of money raised and tell about their adventures. You might want to award your first-place garbage-collecting team with a free pass to the city dump or some other appropriate token. Don't forget to drop off the goods at recycling centers.

Do this project on a Saturday and report back to your church members the next day—and start collecting the real goods!

Trash-a-Thon

Have you had a Trash-a-Thon lately? While not a new idea, it is always worthwhile because it makes the community look better.

Young people get sponsors per bag of trash they will collect, up to 10 bags. Group members can go door to door in the community too; people are eager to give support when they realize how they'll benefit from the project.

When the day arrives, turn the group loose in pairs in parks, neighborhoods, and other areas that need cleanup jobs. After group members have finished their collections, have them report back to their sponsors on how many bags they filled with trash and collect the money.

Truck Wash

Make arrangements with a local trucking firm to wash its big vans for a fee. The firm provides the buckets, soap and long brushes, and you provide the people and lots of elbow grease. It's a dirty, wet and messy job, but you'll make a good profit. Have your camera handy for some great photos!

Weight Away

There are many fad diets to help people lose extra pounds. Here's an idea that not only helps others lose weight but raises money for your group as well.

Conduct a fund raiser for six weeks called Weight Away, which is similar to the Weight Watchers program. Those who take part pay an entry fee and weigh in once a week, usually before or after church. Each time they weigh they pay a fee. An added incentive: Each person must pay a certain amount for every pound he or she gains during that week.

Provide sample diet and information booklets on health and

nutrition for each person who enrolls. Sample diets and helpful booklets are available from most weight clinics, health clubs, health-food stores, local physicians or the local library. Encourage participants to exercise.

You'll need the following materials:

● Scales (preferably a doctor's scale).

● Notebook to chart each person's weight loss/gain (keep the information confidential).

● Small gift (to be awarded to the person who loses the most weight).

Set up a room in your church for this fund raiser. Publicize the event a few weeks before it starts. Stress the importance of having as many people as possible to participate. You may also want to serve fruit juices while people weigh in.

People have fun losing weight, even if it's only for a short period of time.

Window Wash-a-Thon

Combine fund raising, service and outreach with this window-washing fund raiser. Kids can use this clean-fun "thon" to raise money for their special group projects.

First, have group members secure pledges for every window they wash in a Window Wash-a-Thon.

Then set aside a Saturday or two and go through the church neighborhood washing people's windows—free. People will wonder, "What's the catch?" Tell them who you are, that you're doing a community service and raising money for a special project, and invite them to church.

After washing the windows, group members collect their pledges. Your neighbors will have clean windows and you'll have clean money for your project.

Windshield Wash

Here's a fund raiser for a Saturday afternoon.

Arm your group with clean rags and window cleaner and go to the parking lot of a large shopping mall. Offer to clean car windows for a small donation. You'll find a surprising response from car owners arriving and departing from the lot. The cleaning process takes an average of one minute, and drivers may offer tips to the workers to clean the chrome or dashboard. A steady clientele is ensured by shoppers arriving in large numbers throughout the day.

Place colorful posters at the entrance of the parking lot that tell of the project for which the students are raising the funds.

With the decline and expense of full-service gas stations, shoppers are pleased at this low-cost convenience provided by students.

With little preparation and a small investment in spray window cleaners, this innovative idea can turn into a profitable success.

$pecial Events

Bible Costume Party

Advertise a Bible Costume Party through your church bulletin. Start advertising two months prior so everyone will have time to make costumes. Set the party for a Saturday night and sell tickets in advance.

At the party, ask each person to get up and tell a short story about the person or thing he or she portrays.

Examples from the Bible include Goliath, Esther, Noah and Moses. A person with red hair could dress up as the burning bush.

You'll all learn something about biblical characters in a really personal way.

Christian Skate

Every month, sponsor an evening of Christian roller-skating. Rent a local rink from 8:30 to 11 p.m. Use your own disc jockeys and contemporary Christian music. Charge admission.

You'll draw kids from all kinds of churches. Publicize the event with posters placed at schools, churches and shopping malls.

Christmas Crafts Day

Host this fund raiser on one of the school holidays a few days before Christmas. It accomplishes several things:

● It gives parents of small children extra time to do their holiday shopping.

● It provides a morning of fun and learning for 4- through 9-year-olds.

● It provides a model for younger children as they work with teenagers involved in the church.

● It puts everyone in the spirit of Christmas giving.

● It's profitable.

Group members purchase supplies (beads, Styrofoam, paints, ornament kits and so on) for creating homemade Christmas tree ornaments. Young children go to tables, by age, and make at least two ornaments. Then they take their crafts to another table where they are assisted in gift-wrapping them for Mother, Dad or any person they'd like.

The morning also includes Christmas storytelling, carol singing and refreshments. A ticket for the activity is a set fee for the first child in the family, a smaller amount for the second and third child, and the rest are free.

Christmas Crafts Fair

Help Christmas shoppers avoid the mad rush by sponsoring an annual Christmas Crafts Fair at your church. It's a great congregation-oriented activity.

Invite artists from your congregation and the area to partici-

pate in the fair, held the first or second weekend in December. Each artist/craftsman pays a modest fee to rent a booth. The group provides a table, chairs, coffee and doughnuts during the morning setup time.

Publicity is essential. One month before the fair, plaster the community and schools with posters, fliers and news releases to the media and other churches.

The night before the fair, decorate and set up booths in a corner of the church's parking lot. (Churches in colder climates will need to sponsor the fair indoors.)

In the morning, help the artists get their displays ready. Some of the group members don clown outfits and Santa suits, entertaining the crowds and giving candy canes to children. Other members babysit the kids inside the church, letting the little ones color and create crafts while their parents shop for arts and crafts outside. You can also sell coffee and doughnuts.

The artists/craftsmen usually sell lots of their products. The shoppers genuinely enjoy the friendly atmosphere, quality handmade gifts and helping out the group.

Christmas Luminaria Sale

Luminarias are traditionally lighted on Christmas Eve to signify lighting the path for the Wise Men. These little lanterns made from paper sacks are placed along the edges of sidewalks, driveways and roofs.

All you need are paper sacks (No. 3 size), votive candles and sand. Look for a place where you can dig sand for free. Make the luminarias in an assembly-line process. Fold down the top two inches of the bag. This adds stability. Then pour in about an inch of sand and place the candle in the center.

When delivering luminarias to customers, place them about 3 feet apart along the edges of the sidewalks. You can use small torches or railroad flares to light the candles.

For added pleasure, set up luminarias around your church on Christmas Eve.

Christmas Tree Disposers

Here's a worthwhile service and a good fund raiser. Offer a Christmas tree disposal service.

Before Christmas advertise your service of visiting customers' homes and carefully removing their Christmas trees.

Take orders and set up a schedule.

Take an old sheet or bedspread so you can wrap up the dead tree before moving it. This minimizes scattering needles all over the floor.

Once outside you can chop off the limbs and put them in a plastic bag, ready for trash pickup. You can also chop the remaining trunk into 2-foot lengths, bundle them up and sell them for firewood.

You can charge for the tree disposal service or collect pledges from others for each disposed tree.

Christmas Wafers Sale

If you're searching for an interesting fund raiser that helps the poor and needy during Christmas, try selling Christmas wafers.

Christmas wafers are a Polish/Slavic tradition. These wafers are shared among family members before the evening meal on Christmas Eve. They are made of thin, unleavened bread and measure about 6 inches x 4 inches. Everyone is given a wafer (a pink wafer is given to the youngest). A family member then wishes another member a "merry Christmas" and other blessings. The well-wisher then breaks off a piece of the other person's wafer and eats it. The other family member then reciprocates the act.

Sell the wafers during Advent. Advertise the sale through fliers and articles in the church bulletin. Sell packages of four wafers (three white, one pink). Christian supply stores may be able to supply you with wafers. You can order the wafers directly from Christmas Wafers Bakery, Box 99, Lewiston, NY 14092. Its phone number is (716) 754-2399. The bakery offers wafers, envelopes to sell them in and instructions for use in family worship.

Make it clear that the profits will go toward helping needy people during the holiday season. Christmas wafers are a beautiful way of sharing the holiday with the family, church and community.

Comedy Videos

Combine group members' love for media and their creative flair and produce a delightful and effective fund raiser. Kids get a chance to have fun on film.

First, choose a place in your church where people can sign up to have a video made. A small table in the foyer is ideal. Have interested people complete a Video Information Form, leave a blank videocassette and pay a set fee.

The Video Information Form includes a description of the basic plot and setting. For instance, someone's anniversary, birthday party or first date. Have a place to list the characters in the movie, their age and personality type (they're shy; funny; always serious) and then any instructions as far as what sort of conversation took place or order of events. See the sample Video Information Form on page 84.

Take the Video Information Form and make a 10- to 15-minute movie. Set up a special room in your church as the production studio complete with props and backdrops.

Let's say a family in your church lists their cross-country

Video Information Form

Fill in this form as completely as possible. We'll make up any information you don't provide.

People you want in the movie:

Name	Age	Personality type
1.		
2.		
3.		
4.		
5.		

Briefly describe the basic plot and setting you'd like to see in your movie:

Any special instructions, humorous situations or scenes you'd like to see in this movie?

summer vacation—every place they visited, what they did and who they saw. The main characters were a mom, dad and three daughters. One place they visited was the Grand Canyon.

To produce the comedy video, three guys dress up as little girls. In the opening scene they go outside. The father loads suitcases onto the roof of a car and they keep falling off and opening up. A washtub with rocks in it resembles the Grand Canyon, and the family looks down into the tub. Characters do just about anything and everything to make the video funny.

After you've made a number of videos, set a date for a special showing for the whole congregation. You might want to plan a banquet and charge admission. For additional fun, have people guess which family is being portrayed in each video.

Congregational Christmas Card

Writing and mailing stacks of Christmas cards can be tedious. Here's an energy-saving idea.

Make a huge Christmas card by using posterboard, felt, glitter and paint. Pattern it off a regular card. Place your supercard near the front door of the church.

A sign near the card instructs church members to send Christmas tidings to their church friends by simply jotting their greetings on the big card. Then urge them to donate the cost of cards and postage to the youth group.

Generate publicity in the Sunday bulletin, church newsletter and during Sunday announcements.

Easter Basket Factory

Want a new fund raiser? Have your group create and sell Easter baskets.

For traditional baskets, ask each group member to donate a different type of candy (for example, jellybeans, malted-milk balls, marshmallow eggs or chocolate bunnies). For health-food Easter baskets, have the young people donate hard-boiled eggs, bananas, oranges and raisins. Instead of chocolate bunnies, create fruit bunnies: Use two bananas for ears, an orange for the head and use toothpicks to attach raisins for the eyes and nose.

Also include tokens of Easter such as miniature crosses, butterfly or rainbow stickers, balloons, packets of flower seed, and rolled-up scrolls of Easter Bible verses inside colored plastic eggs.

Baskets, ribbon and decorative grass are inexpensive and can be purchased at discount stores.

Gather the group members one afternoon and form an Easter basket assembly line. Wrap the filled baskets with clear plastic wrap, tied securely with a bow. Price the different-size baskets, then begin selling!

Great Pumpkin and Apple Festival

On the Sunday before Halloween, sponsor a Great Pumpkin and Apple Festival. The preparations for this are as much fun as the sale itself.

On the first weekend in October, adult volunteers and young people drive to an apple farm and spend an afternoon picking up 6 to 8 bushels of apples. Most varieties of apples are ripe then, so there is a large selection. You can probably buy apples from a market at a reasonable price, but picking them is more fun.

During the next two weeks, polish and sort the apples. Distribute some to church members who have volunteered to bake cakes, pies, doughnuts or breads (all containing apples). Bag some for sale, and select about 200 to make caramel apples a couple of days before the sale.

Finally, purchase about 250 various-size pumpkins from a local farmer and set them outside the church. Set up tables of the baked goods, bags of apples, caramel apples, cider, coffee, etc., and sell the goods after the worship services and to the community. Apple products are usually sold out; leftover pumpkins are donated to a child care center.

Haunted Maze

Halloween will never be the same again after you hold this fund raiser at your church.

Build a maze by connecting several large appliance boxes.

Each maze section should lead to a haunted room. Have a safari room complete with cave men and wild animals; a spook haven featuring Frankenstein, ghosts and goblins; and a Dr. Jekyll operating room. (For example, have a group member sit inside a box with only his head poking through the top. His head will look as if it is detached from his body and sitting on top of the operating table.)

Charge admission for people to crawl through the haunted maze—if they dare.

Historic Note Cards

This fund raiser combines the fun of Christmas and your local area's history.

Have your group tour and sketch local historic sites on 8½×11 plain white paper. Use pencils to draw the sketches. Later, provide each person with a bottle of black India ink and a quill pen (obtained from a local art supply store). Tell the kids to go over their pencil drawings with black ink.

Next, take the inked drawings to a local printer. Have the printer reduce the group's drawings small enough so they'll all fit on the front section of a folded 4×6 note card. Cut out the reduced drawings and arrange them on the card in a unique display that tells about your city. Have the cards printed on a heavy-grade stock of white paper. Leave the inside of the cards blank; however, print a historic message on the back of each card. Here's an example of what you could print on the back of the cards:

Burlington, Iowa, settled in 1833, is known for the Mississippi River, Chief Blackhawk, the Burlington Northern Railroad, beautiful parks and historic Snake Alley.

Designed by the First Christian Church Youth Group; (list each group member's name).

Take orders about three months before Christmas so you'll know how many cards to order from the printer. Sell cards to church members, local business people, friends and acquaintances.

This fund raiser gives your group publicity. It's also a great way for group members to artistically express themselves.

Hunger Concert

How do you combine kids' love for music, raise awareness about world hunger and get major media publicity for the church? Give four local bands an opportunity to perform and sponsor a concert for hunger.

Locate local bands that will perform gratis or at low cost for a charity event. Discuss the concert with them so both they and you know what to expect.

Contact your church or denominational organization that's concerned about world hunger. Get publicity information and arrange to send proceeds to that organization.

Find a suitable location—perhaps a church fellowship hall or school gym or auditorium. Provide necessary security. Decorate the concert hall appropriately.

Publicize the event through local and school newspapers, posters, church announcements, local radio and TV stations and fliers. Local newspapers and radio and TV stations have public-service budgets for publicity of benefit events.

Sell tickets. Set the price to cover all costs and raise a significant amount of money. But don't make it so expensive that the cost keeps people away.

Make arrangements for soda and candy. Refreshment sales should cover their expenses so ticket sales can go to feed the world's hungry. Secure a good sound system. Assign crews for setup and cleanup of the area.

Then sit back and enjoy the concert.

Make Me Laugh

For fun and profit, put on a Make Me Laugh show.

Buy props (such as disguises and costumes) and prepare a bunch of funny jokes and gags. Publicize the show and invite the congregation. Ask each person who thinks he or she can keep a straight face to put up a minimum of $1. If group members make him or her laugh, they get to keep the money. If group members can't provoke laughter, return the contestant's money.

Group members can let loose with their funny stuff. For example, a group member can "cure" somebody of an ear

problem by pulling cauliflowers from his or her ears. Someone else can read funny news headlines. Another person can do a routine as "Diaper Man."

Everyone will laugh, and so will you as you deposit their money into the youth fund.

New Year's Babysitting Service

Looking for a good fund raiser? Need a group activity for New Year's Eve? Combine the two!

Announce in your church and community that your group is offering a super babysitting service for New Year's Eve. Set a price per child, and ask the parents to drop off their children (with sleeping bags) at the church. They may pick them up the following morning.

Plan all kinds of fun stuff for the kids: games, movies and refreshments. When they have thoroughly exhausted your group, tuck them in their sleeping bags. You may want to divide the kids into age groups.

Serve breakfast for the kids the next morning before the parents come.

This is a fun fund raiser, a good service to parents and a different way to spend New Year's Eve.

No-Show Ball

Are you tired of coordinating events to raise funds for the

youth group? How would you like to raise money for your current project or event while sitting back and doing nothing? Well—almost nothing? Sounds too good to be true.

Try a No-Show Ball. All you do is send invitations like the following for this non-event.

The Youth Ministry
Requests the Pleasure of Your Company
at the

First Annual
No-Show Ball
to Benefit
Our Summer Retreat
Not to Be Held
on Monday, the First of June
This Year.
Anywhere at All
at
Any Time Whatsoever
So Please Don't Come
R.S.V.P.
Sponsored by: The Youth Ministry
(Your church's name and address)

_____ Count on me! Here's my contribution for the summer retreat in place of the new outfit I don't have to buy.
_____ Thank you for inviting me. I'd be glad not to come so the youth ministry can receive funds to help with its summer retreat.

People who support the youth ministry don't have to show up, dress up or find a babysitter. All they do is send a contribution to the youth ministry.

Party Clowns

Do you have a few group members who like to clown around? Why not use their talent to raise funds? Entertaining as clowns at children's birthday parties offers excellent opportunities.

Ask for volunteers to dress like clowns. Dig out old clothes for each clown's costume. Buy clown face makeup kits at a local magic shop or drugstore. (Clown makeup sticks come in water or oil base. Oil base makeup is easier to put on; however, you'll have to remove it with baby oil or cooking oil.) Gather props such as wigs, hats, bracelets, colored handkerchiefs, brooms—anything to make your party clowns complete. Have the kids learn magic tricks and puppetry.

Announce to your congregation that your clowns are available for children's birthday parties. Or visit local preschools and explain your clown ministry.

Print fliers that detail your fee, hours and the entertainment you'll provide. Send four clowns and allow two hours for each party. The first hour includes clowning, a puppet show, games and magic. The second hour includes general supervision, help with opening presents and cleanup. Close with a face-painting session for the children.

Personalized Puppet Shows

Discover a unique approach to puppetry through Personalized Puppet Shows.

Personalize the presentations by finding out the names of people in the organizations where you want to perform. Any general facts about the organizations also help. Then make up your own skits with stories about these people and some of the humorous things that have happened to them.

With that information, tailor the programs to each special audience. Puppeteers will feel an increased sense of enjoyment and ministry as they carefully prepare for each audience.

Write skits and make special recordings for each program. Expenses are mainly the time and talent of the young people if you already have puppets and a stage.

Singing Carol-a-Grams

This idea is a great Christmas-time fund raiser/service project/fun time. Sell Singing Carol-a-Grams to people in the church.

Take orders for three weeks. On the order form include a space where carol-a-gram senders can write a message. Christmas cards could also be provided for the messages. Have the

carol-a-gram senders write a carol for your group to sing to the receivers.

On the carol-a-gram delivery day, split into two groups and go from house to house. Sing a carol, wish the residents a "merry Christmas" and deliver the sender's yuletide message.

Shut-ins and other people genuinely enjoy both sending and receiving carol-a-grams.

Singing Mom-a-Grams

Organize a Mother's Day corsage and singing-card delivery

service! Here's how.

Three weeks before Mother's Day, hang posters and advertise your services with a special insert in your church bulletin or newsletter. Offer either a silk-flower corsage or a mom-a-gram (or both) at a "sale" price. Charge a fee for single services and a higher fee for both, depending on your estimate of the cost of the materials.

Two weeks before, take orders and collect as much of the money as possible. Purchase the silk flowers, ribbon, pins (for the corsages) and card-making supplies.

Then one week ahead of time, get everyone together to make the corsages and cards—and practice singing. The tune to "We Wish You a Merry Christmas" adapts well. If you choose to send delivery people out in pairs, find the best voice combinations.

Deliver the mom-a-grams and corsages on the day before Mother's Day so all the proud moms can wear their corsages on the big day.

Singing Valentines

Just before Valentine's Day, offer Singing Valentines. Customers will pay your group to call their sweethearts and sing them a love song.

Here's how it works. A few weeks before Valentine's Day, spread the word about your Singing Valentines service. Put notices in the church newsletter and put up posters in the high school. Keep your fee small so that anyone can order at least one valentine. When group members take orders, ask for the sweetheart's name and phone number, and the name of a song to be sung to the sweetheart. (Offer a list of possible songs such as "You Are My Sunshine" sung to the tune of "Happy Birthday.")

Then, on the night before Valentine's Day, split up into teams of six or seven and go to an office building with several phones. Then make the calls and explain first to the sweethearts that these special Singing Valentines are sent by so-and-so.

You may want to continue this service for birthdays and anniversaries.

Souper Sunday

Hold Souper Sunday on Super Bowl Sunday and feature four kinds of homemade soup (for instance, chicken noodle, beef vegetable, chili, and split pea with ham), tossed salad with choice of three dressings, dinner rolls and coffee, tea or fruit drink. Charge a fee for adults (free refills of soup included) and a smaller fee for children under 12. Sell large brownies separately. Shop carefully to find the best buys on items for the meal. Group members eat free after all others are served.

Start the fund-raising publicity three or four weeks before the event. Design a sign-up poster with a football Souper Sunday theme and place it on the church bulletin board.

Group members and sponsors meet early in the afternoon for food preparation and table setting. Seat customers at tables. Some group members act as waiters by taking orders and delivering food to tables; the others serve as the kitchen crew.

Encourage church members to bring portable TV sets so everyone can watch the game easily. You might want to borrow or rent a large-screen television to add to the event's excitement. Serve popcorn during the game. Provide board games and other activities for those who aren't football fans.

One benefit of this fund raiser: It helps group members develop a "servant spirit." Preparing, serving and cleaning up after the event and waiting to eat until everyone else is served also help develop this servant quality.

THE JACK O. LANTERN
INSURANCE COMPANY
OFFICIAL POLICY

Spook Insurance

Last Halloween, did your neighbors and friends have trouble with ghosts and goblins? Did they wake up in the morning to find their windows soaped, their yards covered with trash, or rotten tomatoes on their cars?

This year, why doesn't your youth group protect these unfortunate people and earn money?

The "Jack O. Lantern Insurance Company" will sell "a piece of the pumpkin" to individuals who want to insure their dwelling, automobile, property or all three. Prices vary according to the type of policy.

Jack O. Lantern policies guarantee that group members will clean any damages caused as a result of "spooks" on Halloween night, provided they are reported by the specified date.

Start with your congregation, and make sure everyone is offered a policy. Then, each of your members go door to door in his or her neighborhood selling policies.

Your photocopied policy should have spaces for the insured's name and address and the type of policy desired. Use a carbon, making a copy for the insured and for your group.

Then, have teams of two or three kids that can be dispatched to the houses reporting "attacks" from Halloween tricksters.

This is a fun fund raiser and your only expenses are the photocopied policy fliers and a few bottles of cleanser. Plus, you're providing a useful service.

Here's how you can set up your policy:

The Jack O. Lantern Insurance Company
(Set your own price for each coverage.)

Coverage A	Dwelling
Coverage B	Automobile
Coverage C	Property
Coverage D	All perils

Name: _____

Address: _____

Type of Policy: _____

This coverage includes any act in which the following are used: eggs, soap, tomatoes, watermelons, shaving cream, marshmallow cream, toilet paper or trash.

This coverage does not include and specifically disallows vandalism and malicious mischief, meaning only the willful and malicious damage to, or destruction of, the property covered. (Examples are burning, painting and broken windows.)

Claims must be reported by November 2, before 6 p.m.

All cleaning or clearing will be finished by midnight, November 2.

To report claims, call one of the following phone numbers.

_____

_____

_____

Summer Christmas Auction

Try this fun fund raiser! Though not a new idea, it's been successful for many groups.

First, enlist a local auctioneer who will be a good sport and dress up like Santa. Then set your date for sometime during July or August—preferably on a 25th.

Canvass local stores for donations of new items to be auctioned. Tell the store managers what your group is doing, and that at the auction you'll advertise the stores that donated the items. Attach a 3×5 card with the merchant's name on each item while it's on display. And have the auctioneer mention the store each item is from before auctioning it.

Whether you hold your auction indoors or outdoors, decorate with all the Christmas trimmings—tree, lights, garland, mistletoe, nativity scene and gift-wrapped boxes. Play Christmas music in the background. Serve Christmas cookies and punch for refreshments. And don't forget a treat for all the kids from Santa!

Super Bowl Sub Sunday

Here's a fun fund raiser based on Americans' addiction to the Super Bowl. It allows everyone to stay out of the kitchen and in front of the television. Deliver submarine sandwiches to homes on Super Bowl Sunday.

Even with a small group, this project is successful. Starting a month before the Super Bowl, advertise your sub sandwich sale. Announce the sale in church, and sell door to door. Promise that you will deliver the subs before the game starts so that no one will worry about cooking on the big day. (Ease your workload by letting church members pick up their subs after the Sunday worship service. Set up a special "sub-delivery table" in the foyer.)

Charge a fee for a whole sub and half price for a half sub. Use 15-inch rolls and put four slices of cheese, hard salami, boiled ham and bologna in each sandwich. Use a food processor to slice tomatoes, lettuce and onions and add them to the subs. Sprinkle commercial Italian salad dressing on each sandwich. Then wrap the subs in foil.

You just might decide to make this an annual event.

Turkey Taste Testers

Hold this popular fund raiser the Sunday after Thanksgiving. Encourage the congregation to bring favorite desserts and turkey dishes. Contestants may enter one of five categories: 15-year-olds and under, men only, gourmet, quick 'n easy or Mom's home cookin'. Put out the dishes after the morning worship and charge a fee per item for non-entrants, and a smaller fee for entrants. Since it's a contest, give each person 10 pennies to vote with. Put cups beside each dish for votes. Encourage "cheating" by asking people to stuff the ballot cup with change from pockets and purses. Winners are those with the most change in the cups. They receive ribbons and are reported in the church newsletter.

Provide drinks, paper plates and forks. Place chairs in the room but no tables to encourage people to mingle and keep sampling. You can also sell copies of the recipes. Everyone will enjoy the contest.

Valentine Heart Cakes

Here's a new twist on an old, familiar valentine treat.

You've probably seen the small candy hearts with cute sayings on them that most stores sell around Valentine's Day. You can do the same with personalized heart-shape cakes.

Three weeks before the valentine cake bake-off, take orders for the cakes from the congregation. Boost the number of orders by showing good-looking samples. Make small and large

heart cakes. The person who buys the cake gets to add his or her own personalized message that will appear on the cake.

On the weekend before Valentine's Day, the group meets at the church to bake, decorate and personalize the cakes people ordered. The young people responsible for baking the cakes use large and small heart-shape pans. A person who decorates cakes professionally can teach the kids to decorate cakes neatly and with a creative flair. Finally, add the personal messages. Of course, make extra cakes without messages to sell to last-minute cake buyers. Have group members deliver the cakes for a small fee.

You'll get a lot more than money from this fund raiser. You'll have a great time working together, learning new skills and seeing all the smiles when people receive the heart cakes with the special messages.

Wrap-Up Fund Raiser

Looking for a good wintertime fund raiser? Try wrapping presents. Talk to the manager of a large department store, shopping center or shopping mall and get his or her permission to set up a wrapping booth. Then charge shoppers to wrap their purchases while they wait.

You'll need a selection of wrapping paper, ribbon and bows. Have some empty boxes on hand for items that come to you unboxed.

Put wrapped sample boxes on display with price tags. Set different prices for wrapping small, medium and large boxes. Then, when a customer comes with a box to be wrapped, you must determine which sample size most closely matches the customer's, and charge accordingly.

Determine your costs for wrapping paper, ribbon and bows, and then double or triple that, and you should come up with a fair price. Charge extra if you have to furnish the box. And you may wish to offer a fancier wrapping paper for a greater

Gifts Wrapped Here

price.

Post a sign that shows your group's name and the reason you're raising the money.

Try to persuade a store owner to sell you the wrapping paper and bows at a discount.

Before you get started, invite one of the moms to teach group members how to wrap a present professionally.

Have your booth well-staffed so shoppers do not have to wait a long time for your service.

Your Ideas Wanted

Have you participated in a fun, original youth group activity? GROUP
Magazine is on the lookout for creative, unique youth group games, parties,
retreats, discussions, special events, worship ideas and fund raisers.
If your group has an idea, submit it to the following address:

"Try This One"
GROUP Magazine
Box 481
Loveland, CO 80539

You will receive a check for every idea we publish.

Contributors to
Fund Raisers That Work

Len Aalberts
Peggy Adams
Mary Allen
Jim Baar
John W. Baker
Shirley Bliven
George K. Bowers
Larry Bradley
Greg Chantler
Julie Clapp
Robert Conrad
Kirk Dana
Deanna DeBrine
JoAnn Duffy
Matt Fabry
Tim Faulk
Richard W. Ferris
Bruce Filson
First United Methodist Church, Cocoa, Florida
Kari Fisher
Barry French
Sharon Gregg
Randy Gross
GROUP Staff
Michele Grove
Cheri Hall
Gary Hall
Jan Hancock
Linda Hazzard
Beverly Henry
Phyllis Hill
Paul E. Housworth
Don Immel
Ted Johanson
Dave Jones
Alan Kieffaber
Juanita Lee
Paul Lippard
Renee Lofgren
Marylou LoFrese
Mark T. Ludwick

Ruby MacDonald
Cynthia Malow
Naomi Martin
Randy Martin
Rick McKinney
Brewster McLeod
Lynndel Messmore
John Miller
Clo Mingo
Alan Muck
Mr. and Mrs. Dale Myers
R. Michael Naron
Brian Newcombe
Shane Noel
Susan E. Norman
Charyla Olsen
Edwin Ortiz
Marie Paneno
Beverly Perry
Mary Joyce Porcelli
Aaron K. Price
Charlie Price
E. Ashley Rooney
Mitzi Rowland
Sharon Saine
Kenneth Schepel
Margaret Shauers
David Silvey
Keith Stagge
Vikki Stea
Charles Stewart
Carrell Stokes
Larrie Todd
Marc Trueb
United Presbyterian Church, Flanders, New Jersey
Terry Walthall
Don Warner
Scott Welch
Karl Whiteman
David Wiebe
William D. Wolfe
James Yoder Jr.

More ministry-building resources from

Quick Crowdbreakers and Games for Youth Groups

from the editors of Group Publishing

Get over 200 sure-fire meeting openers for your group. Here's a collection of powerful icebreakers guaranteed to get meetings, retreats and lock-ins off to a lively start.

These dandy crowdbreakers get all your kids involved fast. And they're ready in an instant. Simply pick a mixer and start playing.

Kids will get involved fast with—

Knee Sit	Towel Soccer
Back Art	Cinderella Shoe Match
Bumper Bods	Chuckle Chain

Plus scores of other action-packed ideas. Add spice to any youth gathering, large or small, with fun activities from **Quick Crowdbreakers and Games for Youth Groups.**

ISBN 0931-529-46-8, $8.95

Group Growers

from the editors of Group Publishing

Here's an easy-to-use resource that will help teenagers grow closer to each other and to God.

You'll treasure this illustrated collection of 183 proven faith-building meeting ideas—more than enough for 3 years of meetings! Simple directions make it easy for you to quickly organize meaningful activites that . . .

- Give affirmation
- Increase spiritual growth
- Improve communication skills
- Strengthen Christian values
- Build trust
- Foster unity
- Promote teamwork
- Deepen friendships

And you'll get special activites to use for Christmas, Easter, special retreats, parties and outings. Plus, you'll discover loads of original publicity tips to boost interest and attendance.

All group-building ideas have been successfully tested by youth groups across the nation. **Group Growers** is a collection of the best ideas from GROUP Magazine's popular "Try This One" section.

ISBN 0931-529-45-X, $8.95

Instant Programs for Youth Groups 1, 2, 3

from the editors of Group Publishing

Get loads of quick-and-easy program ideas you can prepare in a flash.

Each meeting gives you everything you need for a dynamic program. Step-by-step instructions. Material lists of easy-to-find items. Dynamic discussion starters. And ready-to-copy handouts.

Each book gives you 17 (or more) meeting ideas in topics that matter to teenagers . . .

> 1—Self-Image, Pressures, Living as a Christian
> 2—Me and God, Responsibility, Emotions
> 3—Friends, Parents, Dating and Sex

With all three books, you can keep a year's worth of program ideas at your fingertips.

Instant Programs for Youth Groups 1, ISBN 0931-529-32-8, $7.95
Instant Programs for Youth Groups 2, ISBN 0931-529-42-5, $7.95
Instant Programs for Youth Groups 3, ISBN 0931-529-43-3, $7.95

Youth Ministry Care Cards

Here's a fast, inexpensive way to keep in touch with your kids. **Youth Ministry Care Cards** are crazy, colorful post cards with special messages to lift the spirits of any teenager. Each 30-card pack contains six wild, original designs. Send your kids . . .

- Affirmations—upbeat, positive messages of encouragement
- Attendance Builders—attract more kids to your youth ministry events

There's room to jot a short, personal note. Plus, Bible verses on each card to strengthen your message. You'll turn any day into a special day with **Youth Ministry Care Cards.**

Affirmations—ISBN 0931-529-28-X
Attendance Builders—ISBN 0931-529-36-0

Fast Forms for Youth Ministry

Compiled by Lee Sparks

Here's a lifesaver for busy youth workers. **Fast Forms for Youth Ministry** gives you ready-to-copy forms, schedules, checklists and letters to save you time and effort. In just minutes, you'll have ready-to-use documents that took hours to produce and perfect. Each form is designed to help you better organize and manage your ministry. You'll find hundreds of uses for . . .

- Planning checklists
- Evaluation forms
- Sample letters and more

Make your ministry more effective with this practical, useful tool.

ISBN 0931-529-25-5, $11.95
